Sharon L. Vanderlip, D.V.M.

Fox
Terriers

Everything About History, Care,
Nutrition, Handling, and Behavior

Filled with Full-color Photographs
and Illustrations

BARRON'S

CONTENTS

HISTORY OF THE FOX TERRIER

The Fox Terrier is the most well-known and widely recognized of all the terrier breeds, but its ancestry prior to the 1800s will forever remain a mystery lost in time.

Origin of the Breed

Speculation as to which blend of breeds contributed to the creation of the Fox Terrier, and whether the Wirehaired Fox Terrier (Wire) or the Smooth Fox Terrier came into being first, all remain topics of lively discourse to this day. Although we do not know all the details of the breed's long history, we do know that the Fox Terrier has maintained its distinctive type and character for more than a century.

Literature tells us that at the time of the Roman Invasion of England in 54 B.C., Julius Caesar's legions observed small dogs being used by hunters to chase prey into their dens. They were surprised to see the dogs follow their quarry into underground lairs and remain underground to fight and kill them. This instinctive terrier behavior, called "going to earth," is how the terrier received its name.

Inquisitive, intelligent, and adventurous, Fox Terriers love to play games and hunt. Their keen sense of smell makes it possible for them to find prey in any nook or cranny. No hiding place is safe for a small rodent, rabbit, or lizard!

The word "terra," from which terrier is derived, means "earth" in Latin.

The Fox Terrier of earlier times was admired and valued for its courage and tenacity, characteristics that typify the lively and spirited Fox Terrier we know and love today. From the earliest times, Fox Terriers proved themselves to be wonderful companions, excellent guardians, and hard workers. Quick, strong, fearless, and determined, the Fox Terrier's ability to seek out and kill foxes, badgers, otters, rabbits, rodents, and other small game made it a valuable asset, whether in the farmer's country home, or in a royal palace.

In 1570, an English physician and professor at Cambridge, John Caius, wrote a book about dogs in Latin. In 1557, the book was translated into English as *English Dogges*. In this old work, Professor Caius described what he considered to be the true terrier type, and the Fox Terrier, as a breed, had its first recorded beginnings. Since that time terriers have been documented in countless works and have become known throughout the world for their daring deeds of bravery, their intelligence, and their charm.

Various authors have suggested that the Wire Fox Terrier antedated the smooth Fox Terrier, because original terrier stock in the 1700s was all Wirehaired. (They were also black and tan.) It was not until the 1700s that we learn of white terriers coming onto the scene. According to Rawdon Lee, in his excellent and detailed treatise on the Fox Terrier breed written in 1889, a Mr. Doyle observed an early 1700 painting by the Dutch painter Hamilton in Vienna. The painting depicted flowers and a white dog that typified the terrier of the day. Williams Haynes also reported a 1790 oil painting by Gilpin of a predominantly white terrier owned by Colonel Thornton, named "Pitch." This painting was later turned into an engraving prior to 1810 with the accompanying text: "It would be necessary to notice Colonel Thornton's terriers if it were only on account of his celebrated Pitch, from whom are descended most of the white terriers in the Kingdom." Haynes states that in the engraving Pitch appears to be 50 percent Greyhound and attributes the introduction of the Greyhound to account for the Fox Terrier's color and other characteristics that give the Fox Terrier its special qualities of speed, agility, and conformation.

Somehow, there is a mysterious gap in Fox Terrier history, from the time of Pitch until 1870. We do know that Smooth and Wire Fox Terriers were crossed together in the early days of the breed, a practice that no longer exists. And it also has been speculated that the Beagle, Bull Terrier, Whippet, and possibly some Pointer and Dalmatian may have been introduced into the lineage to create the Fox Terrier breed.

Fortunately, from 1870 onward, we have a well-documented history and a perfect pedigree leading up to today's Fox Terrier. "Old Tip," a terrier from Yorkshire, is said to be the source of all of today's Wire Fox Terriers. Four famous Fox Terriers, from which most of today's lineage is known, are stud dogs "Jock," "Old Trap," and "Old Tartar" and a well-known female, "Grove Nettle." One of the earliest Fox Terrier breeders was Parson John Russell, after whom the Jack Russell Terrier breed is named. From 1812 to 1873 he bred hardy working terriers with dense wire coats.

In 1876, a standard for the Fox Terrier was drawn up and the Fox Terrier Club of England was instituted. It became clear from the onset that quality Fox Terriers were the result of selective breeding, using top-quality animals. J. H. Pardoe showed how good quality in the Fox Terrier breeds true, citing that in 1949 120 of 140 wire champions were descended from Champion Cackler of Notts, and 62 smooth champions were descendents of Champion Oxonian through Champion Splinter.

In 1885, nine years after the founding of the Fox Terrier Club of England, the American Fox Terrier Club was established. It holds the distinction of being the first specialty club to become a member of the American Kennel Club (AKC). For the next one hundred years, Fox Terriers would be registered and exhibited in the United States as one breed.

In 1886, the American Fox Terrier Club held its first specialty show, which was judged by the famous English breeder and judge, Francis Redmond. At that first show there were 75 Smooths and a paltry entry of only 4 Wires. From that time on, the Fox Terrier became an American success story, accounting for more Westminster Best in Show (BIS) awards than any other breed. For example, the 1907, 1908, 1909, and 1910 Westminster BIS awards went to Smooth Fox Terriers. As Wires gained in popularity, they were exhibited in greater numbers and soon outnumbered the Smooths in entries, sometimes as much as four to one. This is reflected in the Westminster BIS awards of 1915, 1916, 1917, 1920, 1926, 1928, 1930, 1931, 1934, 1937, 1946, and 1966—all of which went to Wire Fox Terriers! Today the Wire Fox Terrier continues to enjoy a popularity edge over the Smooths. This is reflected in the AKC registry. Only 848 Smooths were registered with the AKC in 1998 compared to 1,909 Wires. Smooths ranked 86th and Wires ranked 62nd out of the 146 AKC registered dog breeds.

In 1985, the Fox Terrier was divided into two breeds by coat type in the United States in an effort to minimize the number of dogs in group competitions. In all other respects, Smooth and Wire Fox Terriers are essentially the same, except for subtle differences in coloration, markings, and conformation. For example, Wires sometimes have a black saddle marking with a tan head, and Smooths are either black with tan points, or all tan, or have some black shading. Smooths also have wider skulls, a slightly lower ear set, heavier bone, and stand up higher on their toes than Wires do.

Because of its elegance, grace, and charm, the Fox Terrier rapidly took the world by storm and won the public's hearts. It remains today not only the most widely recognized terrier breed, but one of the most beloved.

The Fox Terrier Standard

Today's Fox Terrier standard has remained essentially unchanged from the original standard drawn up in 1876. Height is set at 15½ inches (39.37 cm), slightly smaller for females, and weight at 18 pounds (8 kg). Wires are no longer crossed with smooths, as they are considered to be distinct varieties.

The standard states that the Fox Terrier should be strong, alert, and quick of movement. Expression should be keen and evidenced by moderately small, round, deep-set eyes, and the carriage of the ears and tail. Ears should be V-shaped and fold forward and the skull should be almost flat, sloping slightly and narrowing toward the eyes. The body should be muscular in build and the tail should be carried high and docked to one-quarter of its original length. The coat is dense and so compact that, when parted with the fingers, the skin cannot be seen. The Wire Fox Terrier's coat should be wiry and broken, with hair that twists but is not curly. Coat color is predominantly white (brindle, red, liver, or slate blue are objectionable). (Note: Fox Terriers are usually white and tan or white and black. At birth many Fox Terrier pups have black markings on their heads. This color may last for months, but it is often replaced by a tan coloration later in life.) A detailed description of the Fox Terrier standard may be obtained from the American Fox Terrier Club or the American Kennel Club.

American Kennel Club Group Classifications

Group I	Sporting Dogs
Group II	Hounds
Group III	Working Dogs
Group IV	Terriers
Group V	Toys
Group VI	Non-Sporting Dogs
Group VII	Herding Dogs
Miscellaneous class	

Fox Terriers always steal the show. They have won more Best in Show (BIS) awards at the venerable Westminster Kennel Club dog show than any other breed.

Smooth Fox Terriers are essentially the same as Wires, except for the difference in coat and subtle variations in coloration, markings, and conformation.

The Wire's coat protects it from the cold.

Fox Terriers are energetic, outgoing, confident, and bold.

It's hard to imagine anything cuter than a baby Fox Terrier.

Congratulations to this beautiful Wire Fox Terrier as it wins another Best in Show for the Fox Terrier breed!

It's difficult for a Fox Terrier to sit still for very long! You can train your companion to stay in place until it has your permission to return to its fun and games!

Group IV: Terriers

Airedale Terrier	Lakeland Terrier
American Staffordshire Terrier	Manchester Terrier
Australian Terrier	Miniature Bull Terrier
Bedlington Terrier	Miniature Schnauzer
Border Terrier	Norfolk Terrier
Bull Terrier	Norwich Terrier
Cairn Terrier	Scottish Terrier
Dandie Dinmont Terrier	Sealyham Terrier
Fox Terrier, Smooth	Skye Terrier
Fox Terrier, Wire	Soft Coated Wheaten Terrier
Irish Terrier	Staffordshire Bull Terrier
Jack Russell Terrier	Welsh Terrier
Kerry Blue Terrier	West Highland White Terrier

A good Fox Terrier is the epitome of balance in conformation and character. Confident, social, elegant, and charming, it is no wonder it is fondly referred to as the "Gentleman Terrier."

The Fox Terrier's Place in the Dog World

The Fox Terrier is a member of the Terrier group (AKC classification Group IV), which consists of several breeds of dogs that were bred to hunt and kill pests and vermin and to protect the farm and family. Although terriers may range in size, they are all courageous and bold. Terriers are renown for their busy, outgoing, and investigative nature, and especially for their tenaciousness.

Fox Terrier Celebrities

Fox Terriers have earned celebrity status as a breed. They have been depicted in art and literature since their beginning as beautiful, lively, useful hunters and companions. In the dog show world, the Fox Terrier reigns supreme as the breed that has won the most Westminster Best in Show awards in history. Individual Fox Terriers have made their mark in history as well. King Edward VII owned a Wire Fox Terrier named "Caesar of Notts," and a Wire Fox Terrier named "Asta" co-starred in the old television series "The Thin Man." More recently, Smooth Fox Terrier "Sparky" (owned by David Huffin) has been recognized as one of the highest scoring Freestyle Small Dog Frisbee Champions in the country.

Probably the most widely recognized Fox Terrier is "Nipper," a canine icon of the 20th century. Born in Bristol, England, in 1895, Nipper was given to artist François Barraud when his owner died. The artist observed Nipper's fascination with his cylinder phonograph and thought perhaps Nipper was waiting to hear the voice of his departed friend. Barraud painted a picture of Nipper listening to the Victrola and named the art *His Master's Voice*.

Among the most famous of Fox Terriers is "Nipper," who listened attentively to the Victrola in the late 1890s and who has been the RCA icon since 1929.

He sold the painting to the Gramophone Company, Ltd., and it was used to advertise the phonograph. The Victor Talking Machine Company later purchased the painting, which is now owned by RCA. (RCA purchased the Victor Talking Machine Company in 1929.) Nipper and his Victrola have appeared on millions of record labels, posters, and advertisements ever since.

Countless other Fox Terriers have earned their place in the spotlight, in the show ring, in the obedience ring, and in community service. All of these wonderful animals have done their part to draw attention to their breed and make "Fox Terrier" a household phrase.

But the biggest celebrity of all is the Fox Terrier that lives in your home, protecting and amusing you, and making it possible for you to experience the joy and wonder of the human-animal bond.

SPECIAL CONSIDERATIONS BEFORE BUYING

Now that you have fallen in love with the breed, you must be certain that a Fox Terrier is the right dog for you. After all, you will be sharing the next 12 to 15 or more years with your new companion, so you want to be sure that your lifestyles and personalities are compatible.

Is a Fox Terrier the Right Dog for You?

Every Fox Terrier has its own unique personality, but there are distinct behavioral and genetic (inherited) traits characteristic of the breed that are deeply engrained in these spirited dogs—the same characteristics that have made the breed a valuable asset as a hunter and destroyer of vermin. These include a well-proportioned, small, muscular body, an excellent sense of smell, the ability to move quickly and follow small animals into their dens and kill them, a strong instinct to dig, the desire to bark without reservation, and a dense coat to repel the rain and provide warmth in a harsh climate. This sturdy dog is no pushover.

Fox Terriers are very affectionate, and sometimes jealous. They will insist on lots of love and attention from you, so be prepared to spend a lot of time with your pet.

The Commitment

Whether to bring a new dog into your life and when to do it are major decisions that require serious consideration before you take action. Dog ownership, or guardianship, as many people now refer to it, is not only a joy—it is also a serious responsibility. During the years, your companion will rely on you for love, attention, proper nutrition, training, and good health care. To satisfy these requirements, you must be prepared not only for the financial aspects of responsible pet ownership, but also for the investments you cannot really measure: time and emotion.

The Best Time to Acquire a Fox Terrier

Now that you have made your decision and your heart is set on a Fox Terrier, you need to consider the time to introduce one into your life and your home. You may want a Fox Terrier right now, but there may be other

CHECKLIST

Are You Ready for a Fox Terrier?

Here's a little quiz to help you determine if a Fox Terrier is the right dog for you.

✔ Do you enjoy the company of a dog that is a package of energy, extremely dynamic, and a real busybody?

✔ Are you looking for a dog that is courageous, loyal, and protective?

✔ Can you relate to a dog that has a true sense of humor?

✔ Do you have the patience for a dog that is not only alert and appealing, but is also very intelligent—sometimes to the point that it may, at times, let its curiosity get it into trouble?

✔ Can you forgive your dog for behaviors that may be unacceptable in today's modern world (for example, digging holes in the flower garden or lawn to hunt out prey, and barking), but that were considered qualities for which they were selectively bred centuries ago?

✔ Can you provide enough time and love for a dog that doesn't like to live outside all of the time, or live alone or with other dogs, but has to be with people and is so affectionate that sometimes it is jealous of any attention you bestow on other pets?

If you have answered these questions with a positive response, then you just might be ready to join the ranks of thousands of people who have owned and loved Fox Terriers!

circumstances that prevent you from fulfilling this dream immediately. It is not always easy to find the perfect dog right away. Start by contacting breeders so you can be placed on their waiting list. Sometimes it's hard to be patient, but in the end you will find just the right Fox Terrier, of the variety, age, sex, and temperament you want, and you won't be disappointed.

If you have obligations and your free time is limited, you should postpone your purchase until you will have the time to give the care and attention all dogs deserve. Fox Terriers are bright, active, and extremely affectionate. They thrive on your company and attention, and become bored when left all alone for long periods of time. A bored dog, and especially a bored puppy, is prone to mischief. With no one to keep it company and nothing to do, any dog of any breed can develop unwanted behaviors, including barking, chewing, digging, and destroying.

If you are moving or changing jobs, a new pet can be added stress rather than enjoyment. If you are planning a vacation soon, you will have to make arrangements for animal care in your absence. Rather than stress your new companion by a change in environment and caregivers, it is probably best to wait until you return from vacation before you introduce a new dog into your home.

We all have seen the movies, animations, and advertisements in which a young puppy is wrapped up in bows sitting by the fireplace as a surprise holiday gift. There are two things wrong with this concept. First, it is unwise to buy a pet for someone else. Pet ownership is a responsibility not everyone wants to assume. Second, adding a new pet to the family during the holiday season should be discouraged. This is a time when most people already have plenty to do with visitors and commitments. A new dog can be overlooked in the busy shuffle with all the distractions and excitement. Families do not have time to learn about, supervise, socialize, and care for a new animal during the holidays. Visitors and guests may stress, frighten, or mishandle the new dog. They may even be bitten. Someone may forget to close the crate, a door, or a fence gate and your new friend may escape, be lost or injured, or killed by a moving vehicle. In the holiday confusion, an animal can be overfed or miss a meal, unless someone is specifically assigned the responsibility of feeding. Finally, dogs purchased and transported (especially in cold weather) during the holidays may be more stressed or prone to illness than usual.

Household Pets

Your Fox Terrier ("Anna") is full of energy and curiosity. She has a keen sense of smell and is interested in meeting all the new members of your family, including other household pets. Make sure the introductions are done slowly and safely. For example, if you own another dog

A bored Fox Terrier can get into mischief, including digging holes—a natural, instinctive terrier behavior.

or a cat, don't expect them to be friends at the onset. Your other pets will be cautious and possibly jealous of the newcomer. A resentful cat can inflict serious injury on an unsuspecting puppy. Eye injuries from cat scratches are not uncommon accidents experienced by dogs. And if you have another dog in the home, remember that the dog may be jealous of the attention you are bestowing on Anna, particularly if your dog is an adult or aged animal. Even if your pets are happy to have Anna join the family, be sure that they do not play too roughly and accidentally injure her.

A good way to start introductions in the family is to place Anna in an area of the home where she is safe from other animals, but where they can observe and smell each other. For example, if you have a laundry area, or a space off the kitchen, you can use a baby barrier gate to prevent the new arrival from running loose in the house without your permission until she adapts to her new

Left: Don't expect your newly introduced pets to be friends right away. They will need time to adjust to each other.

Middle: Be careful! A cat's sharp claws can scratch your Fox Terrier's eyes.

Below left: Fox Terriers are very sociable and usually get along well together.

Below right: Your Fox Terrier should always have some form of shelter from hot or cold weather. Never leave your pet outside in bad weather.

A new puppy needs constant supervision. Be sure your other pets don't play too roughly with the new arrival.

There are many health benefits associated with neutering your Fox Terrier at an early age.

Consider keeping two Fox Terriers. They are good company for each other in your absence. Just remember—when you return home, they will both compete for your attention! Twice the fun!

environment and your other pets are used to her. You may also put Anna in her crate the first few evenings so that your other household animals can approach and investigate, but not harm her. Remember to pay extra attention to your established pets so they are not jealous. Remember also that Fox Terriers are very envious of any attention you give other pets and may also become jealous. It will be a real challenge juggling your attentions between your pets and spreading your affection so that they all feel they have received their fair share!

In most cases, animals learn to live together in a household peacefully. However, some Fox Terriers are aggressive toward other dogs that are smaller than they are, or toward dogs that are of the same sex. This is particularly true among male dogs. Often neutering (spaying or castrating) your dogs will help the problem, especially if they are neutered at a young age.

There are some household pets Anna should never meet. These include any small mammals (such as mice, rats, hamsters, guinea pigs, rabbits, or ferrets), birds, or reptiles. Instinct will tell Anna that these small animals should be hunted out and killed immediately. Even a Fox Terrier puppy has a strong instinct to hunt down, dig out, and destroy small prey! Small pets and birds sense when there is a predator in the area. They will be frightened and stressed if their cage is approached. Fox Terriers are very clever and very quick! Make sure the lid or door to your small pet's cage is securely fastened. Then place the cage where Anna cannot find it. Remember, she has a very keen sense of smell and will easily find these animals. Don't just place them out of sight—make sure they are out of reach!

Should Your Fox Terrier Be Neutered?

Fox Terriers are strong and sturdy dogs that do extremely well with tender loving care, exercise, proper nutrition, and preventive veterinary care. One of the most important health decisions you will make is whether to have Anna spayed, or, if you have a male Fox Terrier ("Willie"), to have him castrated. These procedures, called neutering, refer to the inactivation or removal of some, or all, of the tissues in the body associated with reproduction (testicles in the male, ovaries and uterus in the female). Neutering is most often accomplished surgically, although there are also chemical methods that may become more commonplace in the future.

Early neutering can be safely performed on pups between 6 and 16 weeks of age. Studies have shown that prepubertal gonadectomy does not affect growth rate, food intake, or weight gain of growing dogs. In 1993 the American Veterinary Medical Association formally approved of early neutering in the dog (and cat), a procedure many veterinarians and humane organizations have been promoting for years.

There are distinct health advantages for dogs that are neutered early in life:

1. Significantly reduces the chance of developing mammary (breast) cancer if the ovaries are removed before the female's second, and preferably first, estrous cycle

2. Prevents ovarian, uterine, testicular, or epididymal diseases, such as cancer and infection

3. Prevents unwanted pregnancies

4. Less surgical procedure time

5. Rapid recovery period (young, healthy animals heal quickly)

6. Fewer behavior problems

7. Eliminates the inconveniences associated with a female dog in estrus (vaginal bleeding and discharge that can stain furniture and carpets and attract neighborhood dogs)

No procedure is completely without risk or side effects. Your veterinarian will advise you about the benefits and possible risks of neutering your pet.

More Important Things to Consider Before You Make the Final Decision!

Allergies	Some people are allergic to animal hair and dander. Both Smooth and Wire Fox Terriers shed.
Children, the elderly, and physically challenged individuals	Fox Terriers are quick, dynamic, and strong. They can easily topple or trip a small or fragile individual.
Home schedules	Time must be set aside and shared among family members to feed, groom, and exercise the dog on a regular schedule.
Work schedules	Fox Terriers bore easily and do best if they have companionship.
Vacation schedules	Fox Terriers need to be well-mannered, leash-trained, and used to car travel to accompany owners on vacation. Otherwise, arrangements will be necessary for boarding or home care during vacations.
Expenses	Make sure the budget allows for routine expenses (dog food, health care, supplies, boarding) and unforeseen costs (veterinary medical emergencies).
Prepare the yard	Make sure the yard is securely enclosed and the gate latches work correctly. Fence in the garden to prevent digging and access to poisonous plants. If necessary, purchase a pool cover to prevent drowning accidents.
Prepare the house	Select an area of the home to house the new arrival. Make sure the area is easy to clean. Remove anything that is valuable, breakable, toxic, or electrical.
Prepare the family	Make sure the entire family wants to have the dog. Teach youngsters responsibility and respect for animal life, and the proper way to approach and handle a dog.
Responsible dog guardianship	Check into licensing requirements and zoning restrictions for dogs in your neighborhood. Enroll in a dog training class.
Plan for the future	Find a veterinarian. Join a dog club.

SELECTING YOUR FOX TERRIER

The best way to find a Fox Terrier is to begin with your local or national breed association. These associations will be able to provide a list of reputable Fox Terrier breeders.

Where to Find a Fox Terrier

You may also join a breed, or all-breed, dog club in your area where you can meet breeders, dog trainers, and professional dog show handlers who can provide a wealth of information about various breeders. Dog publications, available from your local bookstore or pet store, contain numerous advertisements placed by dog breeders describing animals for sale.

Be sure to purchase from a reputable breeder. Don't be surprised if the breeder you select does not have puppies immediately available. Just remember that a good Fox Terrier is well worth the wait. If you are certain you want to be the proud owner of a Fox Terrier, it is not too early to start checking with breeders today.

A puppy's temperament and personality are well established by 12 weeks of age. Select a puppy with a sweet disposition that is good-natured and friendly.

Puppy or Adult?

Most people want to start with a puppy and there are many advantages to this approach. When purchasing any dog, the most important considerations are the animal's health, temperament, and personality. A dog's personality is well-established by the time it is 8 to 12 weeks of age. By obtaining Willie in the very early stages of life, you may positively influence his adult personality and behavior development. This is much easier than trying to change an established undesirable behavior in an adult dog. However, sometimes, for a variety of reasons, a breeder may have an adolescent or young adult dog available for sale. If the dog has been well-socialized as a youngster, and well-trained, there are many advantages to purchasing an older dog. You can skip the trials and tribulations of puppyhood, including housebreaking, leash training, and basic discipline (such as training your pet not to chew your belongings or dig in your garden). You must be certain, however, that you and the dog are a good match. It is not unreasonable to request a brief trial period when you purchase an adult dog, so that you can be sure the animal will adapt successfully to a new family and change of lifestyle.

An older, well-trained Fox Terrier may be more expensive than a puppy. This is because a lot more time, effort, and expense have gone into the adult animal. Dog breeders often take a monetary loss on the sale of their animals. They raise dogs as a hobby, not as a source of income. The price you pay for Willie will be insignificant compared to the costs you will incur in feeding, grooming supplies, toys, housing, and veterinary care during his life. These costs will far exceed his initial purchase price.

Selecting a Puppy

Once you have decided to buy a puppy and have located a breeder with animals available for sale, make an appointment to visit the breeder and see the puppies in person. Be sure to verify that Willie has been registered and ask for a copy of his parents' registration papers. The breeder can also provide you with a copy of Willie's pedigree. Ask the breeder if Willie's parents have additional certifications, for example, registration by the Canine Eye Registration Foundation (CERF), or any type of testing for freedom of inherited health problems.

Watch Willie in his home environment. Is he happy and outgoing? Is he alert and active, playful and curious? Carefully observe Willie and his littermates for signs of good health and strong personalities. A Fox Terrier is friendly, curious, confident, and eager to investigate. He should not be aggressive or shy. He should come right up to you to investigate, interact, and get to know you.

Next, check Willie's eyes, ears, mouth, skin, coat, and movement. The eyes should be clear and bright and the ears should be clean.

CHECKLIST

Puppy Health Signs

Attitude	✔ Healthy, alert, playful, inquisitive
Eyes	✔ Bright, clear, free of discharge
Ears	✔ Clean, free of dirt and wax buildup, no evidence of head-shaking or scratching
Mouth	✔ Gums bright pink, teeth properly aligned
Skin and coat	✔ Healthy, thick coat, with no evidence of parasites or sores
Body condition	✔ May seem a little plump but should not have a distended belly or thin body
Movement	✔ Normal gait for a puppy, may seem a bit bouncy and sometimes clumsy

Normal gums are bright pink in color. Make sure all the teeth are present and properly aligned and that the baby (deciduous) teeth have fallen out where the adult teeth have replaced them. Sometimes the deciduous teeth do not come out and when the adult teeth grow in there are simply too many teeth in the mouth. Retained deciduous teeth need to be extracted. Check that the skin and coat are healthy and free of parasites or sores. Look under the tail to be sure the area is clean and free of signs of blood or diarrhea.

Finally, ask to see and handle both parents, if they are available. This will help you determine their personalities and give you a good idea of how you might expect Willie to look and behave when he is an adult. Fox Terriers are known for their excellent temperaments and good dispositions. Remember, however, that the way you raise and handle Willie, and the things he is exposed to as a youngster, will have a big influence on his character and temperament. Try to introduce him to people and different sights and sounds while he is still young and can adapt easily. The time you spend socializing Willie as a puppy will pay off a thousandfold when he is a well-adjusted adult.

Male or Female?

If you are looking for a wonderful companion that will keep you entertained and be a faithful guardian, then either a male or female Fox Terrier will do very well.

If you are thinking of raising Fox Terriers in the future, then you will want to seriously consider your options and discuss these plans with the breeder, who can assist you in making an appropriate decision on which animal to purchase at the onset. Most novice breeders begin by investing in the best female they can find, often an adult that has proven herself in the show ring and/or previously produced a litter. Then, with the help of an experienced breeder, the novice finds the most suitable stud dog for the female and pays for its services.

TIP

A Dozen Questions for the Seller

1. Are the pups purebred and registered?
2. How old are the pups and what sexes are available?
3. At what age were the pups weaned?
4. How many pups were in the litter?
5. Have the pups received any inoculations; if so, which ones?
6. Have the pups been wormed or tested for worms?
7. Have the pups had their eyes examined by a veterinary ophthalmologist? If so, ask to see the eye certification.
8. Have the pups been handled frequently and are they socialized?
9. Have the pups received any basic training (housebreaking, leash training)?
10. What kind of food are the pups eating at this time?
11. Ask for a 24-hour health guarantee until you can have the puppy examined by your own veterinarian.
12. Ask to see the parents of the pups.

Occasionally, a Fox Terrier breeder may be willing to part with a well-mannered, trained adolescent or adult dog. These dogs are often ideal for someone who loves Fox Terriers, but lacks the time or inclination to supervise and train a young puppy.

A Fox Terrier should be curious, alert, and sociable. It should not be shy. When you select your puppy, give special consideration to the first ones to come greet you.

Be sure your Fox Terrier is registered with the AKC. Registration is the only proof of your pet's lineage and enables you to participate in official competitions.

Fox Terriers are sturdy dogs that, with tender loving care, can live well into their senior years.

If you are not planning on breeding Fox Terriers, you should definitely have your dog, male or female, neutered as early as possible, for reasons previously discussed.

Age and Longevity

It is a fact that small dog breeds live longer than large breeds, and the Fox Terrier is no exception. Fox Terriers are hardy dogs and with good nutrition and loving care they may live up to 15 years. This is another reason why you should be particular when choosing your companion. Dog guardianship is a long-term commitment!

Registering Your Fox Terrier

One of the many pleasures of owning a purebred dog is pride of ownership and the variety of activities in which you and your companion can participate. For example, without registration papers, there is no proof of parentage or lineage. When you purchase Willie, be sure to verify that both of his parents are registered and that he has been registered as well. Do not confuse official registration with a pedigree. A pedigree is a record of the animal's immediate family members (parents, grandparents, greatgrandparents) that the breeder can provide you. Registration is an official document issued by the national kennel club that is proof that a dog is purebred.

If you purchase your Fox Terrier as a young puppy born in the United States, the breeder will give you one of the following American Kennel Club (AKC) forms:

1. Registration Application

This is a blue slip of paper that indicates the breeder, the litter registration number, the litter birth date, and the names and registration numbers of your dog's parents. There are spaces to write in the dog's name, for the breeder to sign transfer of ownership, and for you to sign as the new owner. Some breeders require their kennel name to be included as part of the dog's name. The breeder can name the puppies before they are sold, or elect to have the new owners name them. Once the registration application is completed, the new owner sends it to the AKC, with the appropriate fee. The new owner then receives either a full registration, or a limited registration (see below).

2. Full Registration

This white slip of paper has a purple border and shows the registered name and number of the dog, its birth date, breed, and color. The breeder and owner are also indicated. This type of registration allows for participation in AKC competitions and events, as well as the ability to register future offspring of the animal with the AKC.

3. Limited Registration

This form looks exactly like a full registration certificate, except the border is orange. It provides the same documentation as a registration certificate; however, puppies born from animals with limited registration cannot be registered with the AKC. Only the breeder, not the owner, can change an animal's status from limited to full registration.

A Personality Test for Your Prospective Puppy

Test	What to Do	Desired Response	Poor Response
Pup's interactions with littermates or other animals	Watch pup closely in its activities, without interfering	Bright, happy, sociable, outgoing, bold	Hides: shy, fearful Fights: mean, aggressive
Reaction upon seeing someone for the first time	Stand quietly until pup takes notice of you	Curiosity, interest, runs up to meet and greet the person	Stays at a distance, refuses to approach, or runs away
Behavior when called	Call, whistle, cluck, make friendly sounds	Attentive, curious, approaches to investigate	Keeps a distance, runs away
Behavior after being petted or handled	Caress the pup and play with it	Wants more affection, tries to follow and attract attention or engage in play	Tries to avoid you, tries to hide, runs away, growls
Reaction to strange, noisy objects	Toss a noisy object (milk container with a few rocks inside works well) on the ground, a few feet from pup	Curious, nosy, and brave, the pup boldly comes forward to sniff and investigate the object	Frightened, runs from object
Reaction to strange, loud sounds	Clap your hands or slap your thighs or squeak a squeaker toy behind your back	Pup comes forward to see what is happening or investigate the source of the noise, tries to join in the play	Frightened, keeps a distance, tries to run away
Response to restraint	Push lightly on the pup's rump to keep it in a "sit" or "lie down" position	Complies (probably briefly!) while trying to play	Growls, tries to bite, tries to escape

AT HOME WITH YOUR FOX TERRIER

You have done your homework, found the perfect Fox Terrier, and now you are eager to bring her home and make her feel comfortable and secure.

Part of your pet's success in adapting to her new family and her new life depends on making sure you are well-prepared for the new arrival. If you have everything ready in advance that you both will need, the transition period will go smoothly.

Your Fox Terrier Comes Home

Ideally, your new acquisition will have been introduced to a travel kennel before you bring her home. A travel kennel makes an ideal portable doghouse for Fox Terriers, so this is an item that you will use frequently, for travel and home. If Anna has a favorite toy or blanket, ask the seller if you can place it in the travel kennel for the trip home. A familiar item will help her feel more secure during the trip and during the next few days in her new environment.

Place the familiar item, or a soft blanket or towel, in the travel kennel on top of a layer of

Fox Terriers have no trouble at all making themselves right at home!

shredded newspaper. Make sure Anna has not eaten for the last two hours so that she is less likely to become carsick and doesn't vomit. The trip home may be the first time she has ever traveled in a car. If she feels queasy, she may drool excessively, so be sure to bring along plenty of paper towels. Allow Anna to relieve herself before you place her in the travel kennel.

Your new friend may protest all the way home, or she may simply sleep. Make a decision right now not to give in to her crying, no matter how difficult it is. Talk to her soothingly but be forewarned! If you hold her on your lap for the trip home, she will not forget it, and will expect you to allow her on your lap during every car trip you take together. When she is an adult she will be larger, stronger, and heavier. It is safer for both of you if she remains in her travel kennel whenever she travels in the car.

When you arrive home, give Anna a small drink of water. Remember that she is probably fatigued from her trip and all of the excitement, so a little quiet time is in order. If she is sleepy, allow her to rest. If she feels like

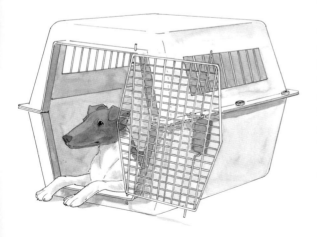

becoming acquainted, do so calmly and gently. Avoid loud noises and sudden movements. Be sure to teach any children in the home to respect Anna's space and privacy. Teach them the proper way to lift and handle her, by gently putting one hand under the chest and the other under the hindquarters for support. Never lift a Fox Terrier by the scruff of the neck or by the limbs. Small children should remain seated on the floor when petting or handling a puppy, to prevent dropping or injury.

Naming Your Fox Terrier

The first thing your Fox Terrier will need to learn is her name. Once she knows her name, you can get her attention and start a line of communication—the first step in her lifelong training.

Your dog's personality will shine through at the onset, so you will most likely have no difficulty thinking of a name that suits your companion and her character. If you need some ideas, you will find plenty in dog magazines and books of baby names.

It seems easier for dogs to recognize names with two syllables. This avoids confusion later on when you give one-syllable commands, such as *sit*, *stay*, and *down*. Names ending in a vowel sound also are easy for dogs to identify, such as "Willie" or "Anna." If you usually call your dog by its two-syllable name, do not shorten it later ("Willie" to "Will" or "Anna" to "Ann") or your dog can become confused.

When you have selected a name, use it often when talking to your new pet. When she

A travel kennel is a necessity for safe travel with your Fox Terrier.

responds or comes to you, praise her lavishly. It won't take her long to know who she is.

Housing Considerations

Today's Fox Terrier prefers the same creature comforts you do, if given a choice. They enjoy living indoors as much as they love to play outside. The most important housing considerations are comfort, safety, and freedom from boredom. If bored or lonely, any dog will get into trouble and develop bad habits (barking, chewing, digging, and scratching).

When you bring Anna home, decide on a safe place (an X-pen, laundry room, area off of the kitchen) where she can feel secure and have some privacy, yet be observed. Ideally, this area will be Anna's permanent housing and sleeping quarters. Take her to her new den to explore and relax for several minutes. Feed her a little treat and praise her. Anna should associate her space with enjoyment. It should be a pleasant place to be. Make sure she can also observe the household activities so she doesn't feel isolated. Fox Terriers are intelligent, active dogs and they enjoy being a central part of everything going on around them. Exposure to various sights, sounds, smells, activities, and people are all an important part of socializing a dog. Remember that Anna doesn't know the rules yet and will require training, so make sure her den is in an area where she cannot chew furniture or urinate on the carpet. Later, when you have started training her, do not use her sleeping quarters as a place to go when she is punished. Her territory should always be a comforting place where she goes when all is right with the world, and not when she is in trouble.

If you have acquired an older Fox Terrier, try to duplicate the previous housing situation as much as possible to reduce the stress of changing environments.

Safety First

Anna will be very curious and interested in learning more about her new home. Some of the characteristics you admire most about your dog—her intelligence, small size, and activity level—also create some of the biggest problems for her safety and make her prone to accidents. Believe it or not, there are countless life-threatening situations in your cozy home.

Convenient Housing Options

Travel kennels	Ideal for use as a small doghouse, lightweight, easy to clean, well-ventilated, provide privacy
Exercise pens (X-pens)	Portable, folding pens, available in a variety of sizes, attachments for dishes
Doghouses	Should be constructed of nonporous material, easy to clean and disinfect
Safety gates	Useful for closing off a designated area or stairway to prevent escape or injury
Bedding	Should be natural material (cotton, wool) because synthetic materials or those containing cedar shavings may cause allergies.

Be sure that you have removed any potential hazards before you let Anna explore and be sure that she is supervised at all times.

Household Cleaning Products and Chemicals

Cleaning products and chemicals are potentially deadly for Anna if she comes in contact with them. Some types of paints can be toxic if she chews on wooden baseboards or walls.

Be sure to keep the seat and lid down on the toilet. Many dogs will drink from the toilet, and if you use any cleaning chemicals in the toilet tank, these can be very harmful.

Antifreeze

Antifreeze (ethylene glycol) is a major cause of animal poisoning. This common chemical can be found on garage floors. It has a sweet taste that attracts animals. Only a very small amount is required to cause severe kidney damage. Survival depends on an early diagnosis. If you suspect your car is leaking antifreeze, do not allow any pets in the garage.

Holidays are hazardous to your pet's health. Your Fox Terrier can choke to death on ornaments and decorations, or it can be electrocuted if it chews on electrical wires. Poisoning from decorative plants and chocolate is also common during the holidays. Make sure your pet is closely supervised and that dangerous items are out of reach!

Rodent Poisons and Snap Traps

If you have any rodent bait that has been left out for wild vermin, pick it up immediately. It is as deadly for Anna as it is for the wild rodents. If there are any dead rodents in the garage or yard that may have been poisoned, discard them. Fox Terriers have an instinctive desire to investigate any rodent they find. If Anna consumes a poisoned animal, she can be poisoned as well.

If you have snap traps set in your house or garage, remove them. They can break small toes or injure a nose.

Electrical Shock

Electrocution from gnawing on an electrical cord is a real potential danger that could cost Anna her life and possibly cause an electrical fire.

Kitchen and Appliances

It is not uncommon for pets to be burned from hot liquids that have spilled from pots on the stove, or from an iron falling on them from the ironing board after a tangle in the electrical cord. Before you do the laundry, check the dryer. Incredibly, some pets have been found, too late, inside the dryer, where they had settled in for a cozy snooze.

Doors

Make sure all doors to the outside or the garage are closed. If Anna escapes outdoors she can become lost and may become the victim of an automobile accident. To prevent a broken tail or toes, be certain Anna is not in the way when you close doors.

Injuries

Everyone in the house must pay close attention to where they step. Fox Terriers move quickly. Anna can dart out from under the furniture and be underfoot before you know it, and be stepped on and injured. If you try to sidestep her, you can also be injured if you lose your balance or trip and fall.

Poisonous Plants

Many ornamental plants are toxic to animals. Fox Terriers have a natural desire to dig. After all, they were bred specifically for "going to earth" and lawns, flowerpots, and gardens are fair game. Keep household plants out of reach and limit home and garden plants to nontoxic varieties.

Foreign Objects

Dogs explore with their mouths and often will eat anything, even if it doesn't taste very good. If something is lying within reach or on the floor, you can bet that Anna will scout it out and sample it. Make sure small balls, children's toys, rubber bands, paper clips, pens, and anything else you can think of is out of her reach. Coins are a particular hazard, as pennies

Be sure to purchase safe toys without squeakers or whistles that can become lodged in your pet's throat.

contain high levels of zinc and can cause zinc poisoning. Be sure that any toys you purchase are safe and do not contain small pieces, bells, or whistles that may be a choking hazard.

Garbage

As unappealing as it may seem to us, all dogs insist on exploring garbage cans. In addition to the obvious hazards associated with this activity, dogs may also suffer from "garbage poisoning," a form of poisoning caused by bacteria and bacterial toxins found in old and decaying foods.

Candies and Medicines

Make sure you have not left any foods or medicine containers within Anna's reach. An overdose of common medicines, including aspirin, acetaminophen (Tylenol), and ibuprofen, can be fatal for her. Chocolate contains a methylxanthine substance, similar to caffeine,

called theobromine that is toxic to dogs. Hard candies can become lodged between the teeth at the back of the jaw or become a serious choking hazard.

Identification

The very first thing you should do once you have brought your new companion home is to be sure she is properly identified. If Anna ever becomes lost, your chances of being reunited are very slim without proper identification. Ninety percent of all lost family pets are unidentifiable and 70 percent of these animals never return home. Annually, 20 million lost American pets are euthanized. Don't let Anna become one of the statistics. If she doesn't yet have identification, stop whatever you are doing and have her identified right now. You'll be glad you did.

Microchips

One of the most recent, high-tech, and efficient forms of animal identification used today is by means of a microchip. A microchip is a microtransponder the size of a grain of rice that is implanted under the skin quickly and easily by injection. The microchip has a series of numbers unique to itself so that each animal has its own identification number. A handheld scanner (also called a decoder or reader) is used to read the identification numbers. Microchips are safe, permanent, and tamperproof. The entire identification procedure (microchip implant or scanning) takes only a few seconds. Scanning is absolutely painless and is accurate.

Once an animal has been implanted with a microchip, the following information is entered into a central computer registry: animal's identification number; a description of the animal; the owner's name, address, and telephone number; and an alternate contact in case the owner cannot be reached. It is the owner's responsibility to update the registry in the event of a change in information. An identification tag for the animal's collar is also usually provided, indicating the animal's identification number and the registry's telephone number.

Lost animals can be identified at animal shelters, humane societies, and veterinary offices. Once the animal's identification number is displayed, the central registry is contacted and the owner's information is released for contact.

Surprisingly, the cost for all of this technology, including the microchip and its implantation, is modest. In addition, the price for lifetime enrollment in the American Kennel Club Animal Recovery database is currently only $12.50. For the life of your pet, this is an investment you cannot afford to pass up.

Collars and Nametags

Another excellent form of identification is a pet collar with your name and phone number clearly written on it. You can also have name tags engraved on the spot at many local pet stores. Collars and tags are easily visible and let others know your lost companion has a family.

Tattoos

Tattoos are a good form of identification because they are permanent. Your veterinarian can tattoo Anna at any age after weaning, usually with only a light sedation. Tattoos are usually done on the inner thigh, although the belly and inside of the ear are sometimes used.

If you are having Anna neutered in the near future, ask your veterinarian to tattoo her at the same time while she is under anesthesia for the surgical procedure. There are tattoo registries where you can send updated information if you change address or telephone numbers. The American Kennel Club's Animal Recovery registers dogs that are tattooed or microchipped.

Housebreaking Your Fox Terrier

Because Fox Terriers are so smart, and like to be very clean, housebreaking is usually accomplished quickly. What's the secret? Patience, diligence, consistency, making sure your puppy gets to the right place at the right time, and lots of praise.

Fox Terriers are meticulous about their living quarters and will do their best not to soil where they are housed or confined. This is another excellent reason for keeping Anna in a travel kennel on the way home from the seller's. If the trip was not too long, she probably will have waited to urinate or defecate. You can start out right by taking her outside immediately upon arrival and placing her right where you want her to learn to do her business. She will immediately urinate, and when she does, praise her repeatedly. You are off to a positive start.

Next, place Anna in her designated living area. This area should have easy-to-clean flooring, such as tile or linoleum, but no carpeting. Remember that she has a very small bladder and does not have full control of bladder or bowels yet. She will need to go outside frequently and certainly will have a few accidents before she is fully trained. But remember that Anna wants to please. As soon as she understands that she should only urinate or defecate in the area you have indicated, she will try her best to wait until you take her to that spot. If she soils in her confinement, it is an accident, so don't punish her. The outdated and cruel training methods of rubbing a dog's nose in its urine, or hitting a dog, is the worst thing you could do. Don't raise your voice or reprimand Anna. She will not associate your scolding with her natural body functions, especially if the scolding occurs long after the act of elimination.

Fox Terriers are very sensitive and scolding a puppy that has an accident is a harsh, unreasonable treatment that may confuse her or break her spirit. If that happens, she may become depressed, less sociable, or withdraw from you. Everything is new and strange to her, and like a baby, she has little control over her elimination at this point. Rather, clean up

---

TIP

Housebreaking Tips
1. Start house training Anna the day she arrives—it is never too early.
2. Let her outside several times a day: first thing in the morning, after every meal, after naps, and as late as possible in the evening.
3. Never scold Anna if she has an accident.
4. Praise her profusely when she does the right thing.
5. Be patient and understanding.

the mess and work on positive reinforcement by praising her profusely when she does the right thing.

Anna doesn't know how to tell you when she needs to go, so for now it is up to you to be attentive to her needs and signs of impending urination or defecation so you can take her outside in time. Signs·include sniffing the ground, pacing, circling, whining, crying, and acting anxious. You must act fast as soon as this behavior begins or you will be too late! Anna will always need to urinate immediately after waking up from a nap or from eating a meal, so in these instances, take her directly outside without waiting for signs. Remember to lavish praise on her for her performance.

Ideally, a young puppy should be let outside every few hours. Of course, there will be times when you simply cannot be available to do this. When you have to be out of the house, or during the night, keep Anna restricted to her living area and place newspapers inside the confinement. She will do her best to urinate and defecate on the papers. Now she has the right idea and is learning to control her elimination until she reaches a given spot, even if it isn't yet the backyard.

Eventually Anna will be able to wait for longer periods of time as she develops more bowel and bladder control. It will be a while before she will be able to wait until morning to urinate, but during that time she will use the newspapers you leave on the floor.

Housetraining is the result of a two-way communication. You teach Anna that she must eliminate outside and she must find a way to

Once your puppy learns where it should eliminate, it will do its best to please you. Be patient, understanding, consistent, and kind in your training. Remember to praise your puppy when it does the right thing!

Wire Fox Terriers require more grooming effort than their Smooth cousins, but the wonderful results are well worth the additional effort!

let you know her desire to go outside when nature calls. She may never "ask" to go outside by barking or scratching at the door or fetching her leash like the dogs in the movies. But if she hasn't been outside for a long period of time, or just woke up, or finished a meal, or starts to pant and stare at you, you know what to do.

Grooming Your Fox Terrier

One of the joys of owning a Fox Terrier is showing it off at its best. Regular grooming will keep Anna's coat and skin in top condition and is an important part of her health care program. Grooming should always be a positive experience for Anna and an enjoyable activity for you. Many Fox Terrier owners groom their dogs as a form of relaxation and artistic expression. It is a documented fact that people can lower their blood pressure simply by touching or caressing an animal. Anna also will benefit from the close human contact she craves and the special attention she receives during the grooming session. She will enjoy the massage sensation and skin stimulation a good brushing provides. Fox Terriers may be prone to skin conditions and allergies. The grooming session is a good time to check Anna thoroughly for signs of dry or oily skin, for lumps and bumps, parasites, burrs, and scabs.

Just as you will require some practice to become skilled at grooming, Anna will require some training to learn how to stand on the

grooming table, what to expect of you, and how she should behave. A few minutes of training in the beginning is a necessary investment, otherwise grooming sessions can turn into frustrating wrestling matches. Because Fox Terriers are so bright, with some gentle guidance and training, it won't take Anna long to learn how to stand calmly on a grooming table. This will make the grooming session a safe and enjoyable experience for both of you.

TIP

Mirror Image

A strategically placed mirror on the wall, level with the grooming table, will help you to observe one side of your pet while you work on the opposite side, enabling you to make sure your pet is trimmed evenly and symmetrically.

TIP

Grooming Table

Here are some tips on how to train Anna to stand on the grooming table:

✔ Be gentle and patient, yet firm.

✔ Use a nonslip mat on the table top.

✔ Start by standing Anna on the grooming table and holding her lightly with your hand between her rear legs. If she tries to move or sit down, apply gentle pressure to bring her back to the right position.

✔ Gently lift and hold each foot for a few seconds until she becomes used to having her feet handled.

✔ Place a brush lightly on her back and sides and then begin to gently brush the surface of the coat.

✔ Remember that puppies bore easily, so limit table-training sessions to three to five minutes.

Preparing for grooming is easy if you follow a few simple recommendations.

1. *Remember that several short training sessions are better than one long one.*

2. Begin training for grooming as soon as possible.

3. Designate an area to use exclusively for grooming. This should be an easy-to-clean, convenient location, close to an electrical outlet (for hair dryer, clippers, electric nail files, or vacuum cleaner).

4. Select a table that is high enough for you to work at a comfortable height, depending on whether you prefer to work sitting or standing.

5. Make sure the table surface is nonslip, to prevent falls or injury.

6. Invest in the best. Purchase quality tools and equipment, particularly brushes, combs, and scissors (blunt-tipped and thinning), and nail clippers. This will reduce your chances of developing blisters on your fingers, or sore wrists and arms from overexertion.

7. Place all the grooming items you will need to use near the grooming table, within easy reach.

8. Use only products designed for use in dogs to ensure a pH balanced for canine skin, including emollient shampoos or spray-on dry shampoos.

9. Give a small food reward at the conclusion of each grooming session.

10. *Never leave any animal unattended on the table.*

The time and effort you invest in Anna's coat and skin will keep her looking in top condition. As you become more familiar with the Fox Terrier standard and develop more skill at grooming, you will find ways to groom Anna so that you can enhance her features to more closely reflect the ideal Fox Terrier.

Smooth Fox Terriers require little more than a good weekly brushing and combing and a nail trim when necessary. However, if Anna is a Wire Fox Terrier, be prepared to spend more grooming your companion and honing your basic skills, including stripping and plucking. Hand-stripping takes longer and requires skill, but the results can be more attractive and the desirable harsh wire coat texture is maintained. Hand-stripping is done by gripping a few hairs at a time rather loosely with the thumb and forefinger and pulling. The dead hair is plucked loose, and the healthy hair remains rooted.

The handstripping technique is more difficult and time-consuming than using clippers, but the final result is more natural and far more attractive.

If you prefer to use a stripping knife, it's easy to do. First, ruff a small amount of the coat with your thumb and leave your thumb under the displaced hair. Next, bring the stripping knife into contact with your thumb, trapping the hair between the blade and your thumb. Finally, pull the hair out with a firm plucking motion in the same direction as the growth of the hair. If Anna is not going to be exhibited, you can save time by trimming her coat with clippers. Clippers give quick results but tend to leave the dull, brittle hair in place along with the fresh, healthier hair. If you are using clippers, use a number 10 blade and trim in the direction of hair growth along the body, removing any stray or straggling hairs.

If you are planning to exhibit Anna, you should consult with Fox Terrier owners whose dogs compete in the show ring. Dog show competitors, professional handlers, and dog groomers can teach you many useful tricks of the trade to enhance your pet's appearance.

Keep in mind that the perfect wire coat takes time to develop and is not accomplished overnight! The average period of time required to grow and build a good coat is around eight weeks. In order to successfully strip Anna's coat, it must be "blown," which means that it must have grown out so that all the coat is virtually dead and stands out from the body, very wavy, so that the strands of hair can be easily plucked out with the fingers without apparent discomfort to the dog. You do not have to strip Anna immediately once the coat is blown. You can leave her "in the rough" for several weeks if necessary until you have enough time to work on the coat to your satisfaction. The entire grooming period can take three to six weeks. The body coat is always stripped off first. Two weeks later, the neck and shoulders should be stripped. One to two weeks after that, the head, ears, front, tail, and rear can be stripped. Don't forget the feet! Neat, trimmed feet look very tidy and prevent hairballs, dirt, foreign objects (such as grass awns), and excess moisture (leading to bacterial growth, moist dermatitis, and sores) from accumulating between the toes. Anna will walk better and track less dirt and debris into your home.

Dental Care

Regular dental care and teeth brushing are very important aspects of Anna's health care program. Without good dental care and maintenance, plaque and tartar can form on the teeth. This formation makes the teeth look yellowish-brown and is caused by bacterial growth and food debris on the dental surface. Eventually the material hardens into a brown coating, starting at the gum line, and with time, covers the entire tooth. The gums also become

A well-groomed Smooth Fox Terrier has a shiny, healthy-looking coat.

red and sore from infection as periodontal disease develops. Periodontal disease causes more problems than swollen, painful, bleeding gums and tooth loss. The bacteria present in the mouth and gums can enter the bloodstream and grow on the heart valves or infect the kidneys and other organs of the body.

The best way to get Anna used to the idea of regular brushing is to start when she is a puppy. Her baby teeth will have fallen out by the time she is six months old, but they are good for practice and training. By the time her adult teeth are in, she will be used to the daily routine.

Purchase a soft-bristle toothbrush and dog toothpaste recommended by your veterinarian or local pet store. Do not use human toothpaste. Many human products contain spearmint or peppermint or other substances that cause dogs to salivate (drool) profusely or upset their stomachs. Use warm water. Cold water is unpleasant and may make the gums and tongue temporarily turn bluish in color.

Start with the upper front teeth (incisors) brushing down and away from the gum line and proceed back to the premolars and molars on one side of the mouth. You may also brush these teeth in a gentle, circular motion. Repeat on the upper teeth on the opposite side of the mouth. When you brush the bottom teeth, start with the incisors and work back to the molars, brushing up and away from the gum line. Repeat on the lower teeth on the opposite side of the mouth. Be patient. You may want to break the daily brushing into two sessions at the beginning. Spend about one minute on the upper teeth and then praise Anna for her good behavior. Later in the day you can spend another one-minute time increment on the bottom teeth, followed by profuse praise.

Good home dental care is a necessity, but it is not a replacement for veterinary dental visits. Even with the best of care, most dogs require routine professional dental cleaning and polishing.

Toenails

Cutting toenails is something most dog owners dread, but it really isn't difficult. If you work with Anna's feet from the time she is very young, she will not mind having her feet handled and restrained. It is important to keep the nails trimmed so that they do not snag or tear, causing pain or discomfort. If the nails become too overgrown, eventually they will deform Anna's paws, interfere with her movement, and impede her ability to walk. In more severe cases, overgrown toenails can curve under and pierce the footpads.

To determine if Anna requires a nail trim, stand her on the grooming table. None of the nails should touch the surface of the table. You will notice each toenail curves and tapers into a point. If the toenail is not too dark in color, you will be able to see pink inside of the toenail, or the "quick." This is the blood supply and just below it is the excess nail growth that

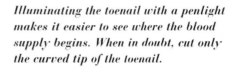

Illuminating the toenail with a penlight makes it easier to see where the blood supply begins. When in doubt, cut only the curved tip of the toenail.

An active Fox Terrier can cover a lot of ground in a day. Check your pet's feet daily for sores, thorns, and injuries.

TIP

Be Footwise

Here is a formula that you can mix and apply to your Fox Terrier's feet to help toughen the footpads and dry sore lesions.
1. Boil 2 cups of water.
2. Steep 10 orange pekoe black tea bags in the water for 20 minutes.
3. Crush 10 aspirin tablets (325 mg tablets) and dissolve them in the tea solution.
4. Add 1 ounce of ethyl alcohol to the tea and aspirin solution and mix well.
5. Allow the mixture to cool before using.
6. Apply solution to affected areas of the footpads 3 to 4 times daily until lesions are healed. (If the lesions are raw or open, omit aspirin from the solution).
7. This solution will keep for several months when stored in a tightly closed jar.

you will remove. If Anna's toenails are too dark to differentiate where the quick ends, you can illuminate the nail with a penlight or a flashlight to find the line of demarcation where the blood supply ends.

There are different types of nail trimmers available. Most Fox Terrier owners prefer the guillotine style clippers. To use these you place the toenail inside the metal loop, aligning the upper and lower blades with the area you wish to cut, and squeeze the clipper handles. A good rule of thumb is to cut only the very tip of the toenail. If the nail is still too long, continue to remove the end of the nail carefully in small increments. If you accidentally cut too close, you can stop the bleeding by applying styptic powder (a yellow clotting powder commercially available from your pet store or veterinarian) or by applying pressure with a clean cloth to the toenail for five minutes.

When the blades become dull, they should be replaced so they do not break, shred, or crack the nails. You may also opt to purchase an electric toenail filer to round off and smooth the nails after trimming. Be sure to praise Anna for her cooperation. Without it, nail trimming is virtually impossible!

Exercise

Exercise is an important part of all Fox Terriers' physical and mental health. Fox Terriers are by nature very dynamic, busy, active, investigative dogs. They enjoy interesting outings and if left alone for long periods of time, they bore easily or get into mischief.

One of the many reasons Fox Terriers are so popular is their practical size. But don't be fooled! Although a Fox Terrier might fit in a small apartment, this is a high activity level breed with a love of the wide open spaces. Fox Terriers need lots of space to run and play. It's up to you to develop a healthy exercise program suitable for her age, stage of development, health, and physical abilities. Anna can have the biggest backyard in the neighborhood, but if left alone all day, she will not exercise on her own. She just might, however, dig up the flower garden!

When you begin to plan Anna's exercise program, remember that she first needs to build up endurance gradually. This requires a regular routine that, over time, may increase in length or vigor. Whatever you do, do not take Anna out for infrequent, strenuous exercise. Start with a moderate exercise program and build it up gradually to a level suitable for her age and health condition. Fox Terriers sometimes just don't know when to stop and will let their enthusiasm take them to their physical limits. You need to know when to call time-out. It's not unusual for a Fox Terrier to play hard until it drops. Don't let Anna reach this point!

A regular exercise program will improve Anna's cardiovascular endurance and function, build strong bones and joints, and develop muscles and muscle tone. Before you start an exercise program, have her examined by your veterinarian and ask for exercise activity recommendations tailored to her needs and abilities.

Exercise Activities for Your Fox Terrier

Walking or jogging is a great form of exercise. It is also strenuous, so start with short walks each day and gradually increase the distance or speed. Anna's natural pace is different from your own, and is usually a very fast one! Her outings will keep you both in shape! Try to exercise on a soft surface, such as a lawn or the beach. Sidewalks and asphalt are hot, uncomfortable, and hard on the joints upon impact. Rocky or gravel surfaces are also hard on the feet. Be sure to check Anna's feet for burrs, torn toenails, cuts, or abrasions at the end of every walk. Treat any sores and discontinue the walks until the lesions have completely healed. If you live in an area with snow, don't walk Anna on salted roadways and be sure to rinse her feet after each walk so she doesn't develop salt burns. Finally, try to walk on level surfaces, especially if she is young and still in her developmental growth phase, or if she is older, or suffering from arthritis. Climbing hills and stairs can be very hard on growing bones and joints or aged hips and joints.

Swimming is one of the best forms of exercise. It builds stamina and works most of the muscles in the body. Swimming is particularly good for older animals because it allows for exercise without impact or trauma to aged joints and bones. Never leave Anna unattended in the water. If she swims in a pool, be certain she knows where the stairs are and train her how to get out of the pool. Be sure also that she does not become chilled. Rinse out any saltwater or chlorine from her hair and dry her thoroughly after each swim.

Fetch is a game enjoyed by many Fox Terriers. They will retrieve objects for their owners, although they are not always willing to immediately give them back! You can use a wide variety of interesting objects for this game, including balls, flying disks, and dumbbells.

Tracking comes naturally to Fox Terriers because they have a powerful sense of smell. If you want to make an interesting game for Anna, try hiding little tidbits around the yard for her to find. You can make the game more complicated by hiding the treats one to two hours in advance of the search and increasing the distance between treats. The advantages to this type of exercise are that they encourage your pet to be active, increase her tracking ability, and you can set the course at your leisure. If Anna seems to have a natural ability for this game, you might consider contacting the American Kennel Club for a Tracking Regulations brochure. Anna might be a candidate for earning a Tracking Dog title!

Make sure you exercise your companion on a flat surface, especially if it is very young or very old. Hills, stairs, and slopes can be hard on growing bones or arthritic joints.

Never give your Fox Terrier old clothing or shoes for toys. Your dog will think any article of clothing, new or used, is fair game! Even a garden glove is a treasure not to be shared!

Good chew toys stimulate gums and help reduce tartar buildup on teeth.

Dangerous Toys	Risks
Rawhide formed into bone shapes	"Knots" of rawhide or other shapes can obstruct the trachea
Latex toys, rubber toys, cotton ropes, hard plastic toys	May shred or break and obstruct the gastrointestinal tract
Toys small enough to be swallowed	May obstruct trachea or gastrointestinal tract

Toys

Fox Terriers love interesting toys, but they play rough with them! No matter what the purpose of the toy you purchase (for example, a ball to chase or a Frisbee to fetch), Anna will most certainly end up chewing on it. It seems all dog toys end up as chew toys, whether designed for that purpose or not. With this in mind, you should always be sure the toys you buy are durable and safe.

Chew toys can enrich Anna's life by providing stimulation of the gums and exercise of the jaws, as well as helping to pass the time and avoid boredom when you are not home. Some chew toys help reduce tartar buildup on the teeth. Chew toys are useful tools to help keep Anna from chewing on valuables, such as furniture or clothing. Never give her an old shoe or piece of clothing as a chew toy. She will not know the difference between an old, discarded item and your most expensive clothing or shoes. By allowing Anna to chew on old shoes, you send the message that anything in your closet is fair game. Don't confuse her!

Not all toys are suitable for Fox Terriers. For example, cow hooves, available as chew toys in local pet stores, are very hard and may actually

Your Fox Terrier may live indoors, but it loves the wide-open spaces. When you are away, your pet will eagerly await your return and expect a stimulating walk or a game of fetch to make up for lost time during your absence.

TIP

Choose Toys Wisely

The best toys are those that cannot break or shred, are too big to be swallowed, and can provide dental prophylaxis (gum stimulation and removing tartar buildup on the teeth).

Train Smart

✔ Keep grooming sessions brief and always end on a positive note.

✔ When Willie requires a reprimand, use the word *no* consistently.

✔ Never use Willie's name in connection with a reprimand.

✔ Always praise him for good performance and behavior.

✔ Train by using positive reinforcements (praise or food rewards) and not by negative reinforcement (scolding, physical punishment).

cause a tooth to fracture. Other toys may break, shred, or tear and become lodged in the airway passages or gastrointestinal tract.

Travel Can Be Fun

Fox Terriers love to travel and a well-mannered Fox Terrier makes a wonderful ambassador for the breed. Whether you are on a long vacation, or a short outing, the company of a Fox Terrier can make the trip all the more fun.

There are a few basic guidelines you need to keep in mind to ensure the safety and enjoyment of your travels.

1. Make sure Anna is trained to her travel kennel and feels comfortable and secure inside of it. This training begins early in life by using the travel crate daily as a security den and placing food tidbits in it periodically. When it comes time to take a trip, she will feel at home in her travel kennel and will not be stressed or fret.

2. Obtain a health certificate for travel. Make sure Anna is in excellent health and able to make the trip. Ask your veterinarian to conduct a physical examination and verify that all necessary vaccinations are up-to-date. Ask if any special medications for the trip are recommended (for example, medication for the prevention of heartworm in certain states, or medication for car sickness).

3. Make sure you have all the things you will need during the trip, including items in case of illness or emergency.

✔ Travel kennel

✔ Collar with identification tag and leash

✔ Dishes, food, and bottled water

✔ Medications

✔ First aid kit

✔ Toys and bedding from home

✔ Grooming supplies

✔ Clean-up equipment: pooper scooper, plastic bags, paper towels, and carpet cleaner

✔ Veterinary records and photo identification

4. Make reservations in advance. Check with hotels or campgrounds to be sure pets are permitted. Reserve space for a dog with the airlines if air travel is part of your travel plans.

If you are traveling by air and Anna is accustomed to her travel kennel, tranquilizers are seldom necessary for air travel, are sometimes ineffective, and are often discouraged. Unless Anna is very young, and small enough to fit under the seat in front of you in a travel case, she will be assigned a space in the cargo hold. Be sure to make advance reservations, as there are a limited number of animals that may travel on a given flight, either in the cabin or in the cargo hold. The cargo hold is temperature controlled and pressurized just like the cabin in which you travel. Don't worry about your traveling companion; she will probably sleep better on the plane than you will!

If your plans include travel by car, remember that some dogs have a tendency to become carsick. To reduce the likelihood that Anna will become carsick, limit her food and water three hours before travel begins and place her crate where she can see outside of the car. Although dogs become carsick from anxiety about travel, tranquilizers are not always effective in preventing carsickness. Another option you may wish to discuss with your veterinarian is the use of an antihistamine (Antivert, meclizine) that has been shown to be effective for some dogs.

Most important: Remember to never leave your Fox Terrier in a parked car on a hot day, even for a few minutes. The temperature inside of a car, with the windows cracked open and parked in the shade, can quickly soar past 120°F (49°C) within a few short minutes and your pet can rapidly die of heatstroke.

Children and Fox Terriers

The Fox Terrier's appeal spans all age ranges. Children are drawn to the Fox Terrier for its endearing appearance and small size. But children must be taught to respect these animated and spirited dogs and to resist the temptation to touch until the dog has had time to become acquainted. The Fox Terrier is an affectionate, joyful, and extremely sociable dog that deserves to be handled kindly. Be sure to teach children to approach Anna gently and to pet her only with permission and under your supervision. Fox Terriers are not aggressive and are very good with children, but nevertheless,

under the wrong circumstances, accidents can happen. The first thing children should learn about any pet is to not put their face up close against the animal. It is very tempting to rub a cheek across the soft fur, or even try to kiss the animal, but this is the one thing they must not do. Because small children are short and their heads are large in proportion to their bodies, the majority of all animal bite wounds inflicted on children (regardless of animal species) happen in the area of the face and head.

With adult guidance, there is no limit to the things children can learn from a Fox Terrier. These wonderful dogs provide an excellent opportunity for adults to teach children about pets, the importance of humane care and treatment, and respect for life. They provide a way for very young children to learn responsibility by participating in the animal's care, learning the importance of fresh water, good food, a clean home, and a kind heart. Older children can learn a lot about animal behavior and biology, training, exhibiting, and respect for animal life. A Fox Terrier makes a dear, trustworthy friend for a child, serving as a confidant and a subordinate—something children rarely find. For a growing child, these are precious gifts that help develop confidence and character.

Some children are frightened or uncomfortable around dogs, especially large ones. Because a Fox Terrier is small and appealing, it can make it possible for a child to replace anxiety, fear, or timidity with tenderness and affection. Adult supervision is necessary when a child is caressing any dog of any breed.

Even children who are somewhat shy often will talk freely when they are in the presence

Always take a leash with you when you travel with your pet.

Fox Terriers make loyal guardians and devoted friends, for children and adults.

When you travel out-of-state, remember to ask your veterinarian for an official health certificate. Also ask your veterinarian about any prescription medications (such as heartworm preventative) that might be necessary for the trip.

When your Fox Terrier has to travel, remember to take along its favorite toy or blanket. A cozy, familiar blanket will keep your companion clean and comfortable. It also helps prevent homesickness in young puppies traveling alone.

Your Fox Terrier will easily work its way into your heart and become an important member of your family.

of animals. A Fox Terrier can open doors of communication and learning for a child. While watching the animal at play, or taking it on a walk, a child becomes a captive audience and a good learner. Together you and a child can share thoughts and ideas about animals, people, families, and anything else you can relate to Fox Terriers and humans on the child's level.

Animal Life and Death

The most difficult thing about owning and loving a pet is the knowledge that even with the very best of care, old age or illness, and eventually death, cannot be avoided. Because Fox Terriers have a relatively long life span compared to other kinds of pets, you and your family will have developed a long friendship and a deep attachment to this canine family member over the years. Children are very sensitive to issues of animal life and death, and the death of a family pet may be the first loss a child experiences. When the time comes to say goodbye to a longtime companion, children are as grief-stricken, if not more so, than adults.

It is very important that the child is prepared in advance for the eventual, and inevitable, loss or death of a beloved pet. It is especially important that this preparation be provided in a compassionate manner appropri-

ate for the child's age and level of maturity. The loss of a pet is a very emotional experience for a child. But if handled skillfully, this loss can be turned into a positive learning experience. It provides an opportunity in which you may openly discuss life, love, illness, or death and possibly address additional fears or concerns the child may have. The sadness from the loss of one special Fox Terrier will be outweighed by the important role it played as a family member helping a child grow, mature, and strengthen in character.

For Wires

1. Chalk all the parts of the coat to be stripped. You can do this by rubbing chalk powder in the coat in all the areas you plan to strip. This helps dry the oils from the coat and makes it easier to grasp the hairs.

2. Brush out the entire coat with a slicker brush. Brush the body hair in the direction of hair growth, from the shoulders to the tail. Brush the chest hair down, toward the table, and the leg hair (furnishings) up, toward the body. Brush the belly hair.

3. Comb the entire coat with a wide-toothed metal comb. Gently work out any small mats with your fingers, then comb through them. In order not to damage the furnishings and undercoat, insert the comb diagonally into the hair and then raise it perpendicular to the ground and comb through the coat without withdrawing the teeth of the comb.

4. Strip from the withers to the base of the tail, down the side of the body to a line not lower than the elbow, along the flank, and to the hips. Do not remove the hair on the chest. You may use the hand-stripping technique described above, or you may use a stripping knife, or clippers. If you make a mistake and remove too much hair, don't panic. The hair will grow back. However, some parts of the coat will grow faster than others.

5. The head and ears are sensitive areas to strip and should be trimmed two weeks after the body is trimmed by carefully plucking out the hair with your fingers. Be careful not to pinch the skin. The head should be made to look as long and clean as possible. Clip the front and back of the ears with a number 10 blade and remove excess hair on top of the muzzle with thinning shears. Comb the eyebrows directly forward to include the beard and trim the outer edges of the eyebrows so they are level with the side of the head.

6. The front, tail, rear, and backs of legs should be trimmed two weeks after the head and ears. Leave a clearly defined fringe on the forepart of the legs, curving back to just above the hock. Hocks should be trimmed to appear round and straight. From the rear, the hind legs should be clearly defined and have a clean, archlike appearance. Be careful not to remove too much hair from the hindquarters (the "drop" or "skirt"), because it will take months to return.

7. Comb the hair up from in between the toes and trim

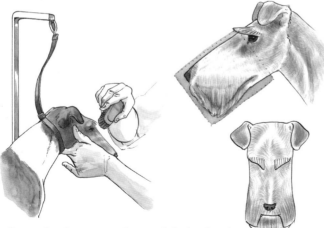

Be gentle when you work around the head and ears. These are sensitive areas. When you use sharp instruments, such as scissors, be careful when you work around your pet's eyes.

the feet with scissors so that they look round and compact. Finally, comb the underchest and trim it to follow the contour of the body. Use thinning shears to give a smoother, blending effect.

8. After stripping and trimming is completed, you may bathe your pet in a mild emollient shampoo to remove dander and keep the skin healthy.

For Smooths

Compared to the Wire Fox Terrier, the Smooth is easy to groom, but it still requires some time and effort. Remember, this Fox Terrier's coat is *smooth,* not *short.* This means that there will be places where the hair grows quite long if left unattended. To keep a Smooth presentable, you must use a stripping knife, single-edged thinning shears, and, in some places, an electric clipper.

The principle areas to trim are:

✔ The frill along each side of the neck
✔ The long hairs on the backs of the front legs
✔ The chest
✔ The backs of the hindlegs from the rump to the hocks
✔ The back of the tail
✔ Anywhere long hairs appear to be out of place

Smooths shed just like Wires do, so the more you groom your Smooth, the less hair you will find on your clothing, carpet, and furniture.

For regular grooming, use a good, stiff bristle brush and brush vigorously. Then use a quality metal comb with closely spaced teeth to work in the direction of coat growth. Finally, strip in the direction of coat growth

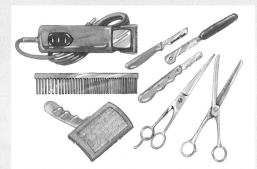

You don't need a vast assortment of grooming tools to keep your Fox Terrier looking its best, but you do need the basics. Invest in the best tools you can afford. Good tools are a pleasure to use, make grooming easier, and produce better results.

and use the thinning shears with the lie of the coat, never against it. If you use the clippers, use a #15 blade, again with the lie. Avoid trimming whiskers unless absolutely necessary. Whiskers are sensory vibrissae that help your Fox Terrier find its way about, especially in the dark, through sense of touch. Although they are often removed for exhibition, if your companion is not on the show circuit, it's best to leave the whiskers alone.

Done properly, regular grooming will avoid the need for frequent baths and keep your Smooth looking much sleeker than you might imagine. If your Smooth happens to get very dirty digging or playing, you can clean her up with a no-rinse, or dry, dog shampoo and a vigorous rubdown with a towel. Follow this up with a few sprinkles of cornstarch and brush out the excess. The whole procedure is quick and easy, and you'll be pleased with the results!

FEEDING YOUR FOX TERRIER

Good nutrition has been recognized for centuries as being one of the most important factors in maintaining health and extending longevity. Of all the countless things you do for your Fox Terrier, providing a nutritionally complete and balanced diet is one of the most important ways to keep your dog healthy throughout life.

When dogs were first domesticated, their meals consisted of remains from the hunt, vegetables from the garden, and whatever "table scraps" were available. Dogs essentially ate much of the same foods as their owners. Due to the wide variety of foods in their meals, most of the nutritional bases were covered. Commercial dog food was to make its appearance thousands of years later. Dry kibble became popular during World War II when meat became a scarce commodity. Later, with consumer convenience in mind as people became more pressed for time, and particularly in the past 40 years, we witnessed the evolution of TV dinners, microwavable meals, and fast-food restaurants. The dog food business

Mealtime is one of your pet's favorite times of day. A Fox Terrier will do anything to remind you that it's time to eat! It takes quality nutrition to keep a busy Fox Terrier in top condition.

was not far behind, ready to capitalize on modern-day lifestyles. It was obvious that families who spent less time cooking for themselves, were unlikely to cook for the family dog. Through advertising and excellent marketing strategies, the convenience of canned or packaged commercial dog food was promoted until it became commonplace. Today the manufacture of pet food is a $15 billion industry. As with all businesses, success is measured by profit. This brings us to a key point to keep in mind as we review nutritional choices. Quality nutrition should not cost a fortune, but it certainly is not cheap.

The important role proper nutrition plays in a dog's life cannot be overemphasized. It is one aspect of health care in which you have full control and where you cannot afford to cut corners. It is the main key to overall health, development, and life span. With this in mind, let's discuss the kind of nutrition Willie requires.

Starting Off Right

Before you bring Willie home, ask the breeder what type of dog food he is currently eating and be sure to obtain at least a two-week supply of the food. Continue feeding the same diet, at least until he has had a chance to adjust to the new family and home. A change in diet during this time of adaptation can be stressful and possibly cause stomach upset or diarrhea. Be sure to take Willie to your veterinarian within 48 hours of purchase for a physical examination and to plan a complete health care program. The first veterinary visit is an ideal time to discuss specific nutritional requirements and the breeder's recommendations. If a change in diet is appropriate, make the change gradually by increasing the amount of the new diet and decreasing the amount of the old diet in small increments each meal.

Nutritional needs will change throughout life, so it makes sense that Willie's diet will also need to be changed at times. For example, when he is just a puppy, he will need a dog food that provides complete and balanced nutrition for growth and development. As he reaches adolescence, his dietary requirements may lessen or increase, according to his individual needs and activities. When Willie is an adult, he will have greater nutritional requirements if he is active, doing obedience work, on the show circuit, or being used for breeding purposes, than he would have if he were sedentary. Finally, as Willie ages, or if he becomes sick or is recovering from an illness, he will need a diet based on his health condition and special needs.

Environment also plays an important role in dietary requirements. If Willie spends a lot of time outdoors in cold weather, he will have a higher caloric requirement to maintain his normal weight than if he stays indoors in a heated building most of the time.

Finally, genetics can influence a dog's caloric requirements, ability to digest and metabolize certain foods, and ability to maintain a normal weight. If some of Willie's family members have difficulty maintaining an appropriate weight (if they are overweight or underweight), this may be an inherited tendency and you will have to make a special effort to closely monitor his food source and intake.

For each of Willie's life stages, you should consult your veterinarian to learn which type of dog food would be most beneficial. The ideal nutrition for him today may not be suitable later in life. With increasing consumer awareness, dog food manufacturers will certainly make greater efforts to maintain a competitive edge and offer the dog owner a larger, more-improved selection of dog foods from which to choose. For these reasons, nutrition will always be an important topic of discussion each time you visit your veterinarian.

Interpreting Dog Food Labels

Today there are countless brands and types of commercial dog foods from which to choose. Many claim to be the best food you could possibly offer your pet. But how can you be sure? Dog food comes in all sizes, colors, shapes, and consistencies (dry kibble, semi-moist, moist canned). You cannot help but notice how many brands are packaged and named to look and sound more like food for humans than for dogs. This is because the marketing is aimed at you, the consumer. But you are shopping for your dog and he doesn't care what color his food is. He does care how it tastes and smells. Even if you buy a very nutritious dog food, it will not benefit Willie if he refuses to eat it. On the other hand, you don't want to feed an inferior formulation that is not nutritionally balanced simply because he likes the flavor. Sometimes the palatability and aroma that appeal to a dog are due to food additives, rather than nutrients (for example, artificial flavorings).

Anyone who has looked at dog food labels will agree that they can be confusing. A good way to select the best dog food is to consult with your veterinarian and Fox Terrier breeders. Another way is to study the dog food labels and select a premium dog food that provides complete and balanced nutrition from high-quality protein sources.

Here are some definitions to help you decipher and interpret dog food labels when selecting the best dog food formulation for your pet.

Ingredients are any of the materials used to manufacture a dog food mixture (proteins, fats, carbohydrates, vitamins, minerals) or non-nutritional food additives (artificial coloring and flavorings, food preservatives). Ingredients are listed on the dog food label by decreasing order of preponderance by weight.

The list of ingredients provides general information about the types of ingredients found in the dog food, but it does not tell you about the quality, digestibility, or nutrient availability of the ingredients. Because different dog food manufacturers may use the same types of ingredients, but differ in the quality of the ingredients they use, do not rely solely on the comparison of ingredient labels on dog food packages to select dog food.

A nutrient is a substance eaten in order to maintain life. Some nutrients produce energy (sugars, amino acids, and fatty acids). Other nutrients do not produce energy (water, oxygen, vitamins, and minerals).

The nutrient profile indicates the type and quantity of nutrients present in the dog food mixture.

The nutritional adequacy (for example, "complete and balanced nutrition") of all dog foods (except treats and snacks) must appear in a statement on the product label. Current American Association of Feed Control Officials (AAFCO) regulations require nutritional adequacy be substantiated by either feeding trials or by meeting the AAFCO Nutrient Profile. Although feeding trials are the preferred method to demonstrate nutritional adequacy in a dog food, the more commonly used method is to calculate the formulation for the diet using a standard table of ingredients, without conducting laboratory analyses or feeding trials.

Protein quality is arguably the most important health factor in a dog's diet. Dietary protein may come from plant or animal sources; however, not all proteins are created equally. In general, high-quality animal source proteins provide a better amino acid balance for dogs than proteins from grains. There is a big difference between a high percentage of protein in the diet and high protein quality.

Some animal protein sources found in commercial dog foods include beef, chicken, lamb, fish, and eggs. However, just because the protein comes from an animal source does not necessarily indicate it is of high nutritional value. You must read the ingredient label closely and look for words such as "meat," "meal," and "by-products." Meat means muscle

and skin, with or without bone. Meal indicates the protein source has been ground or reduced into particles. By-products include heads, feet, guts, and bone. By-products are usually a poorer and less expensive protein source.

Fats are important ingredients in the daily diet. Fats not only add to the flavor and palatability of the food, but they are necessary for many aspects of an animal's health, can play critical roles in clinical nutrition and therapeutic remedies, and influence skin and coat condition. Fats also aid in digestion, provide energy, and are required for the assimilation of fat-soluble vitamins A, D, E, and K. The various fats (animal fat, vegetable oils, olive oil, fish oils) each have different effects on the body.

Carbohydrates are sugars, starches, and fibers. They are an inexpensive source of energy compared to high-quality protein. *Researchers have not yet determined the exact amount of carbohydrates required in the*

canine diet, yet carbohydrates make up the major portion of today's commercial dog foods. These carbohydrates are usually provided in the form of corn, corn meal, rice, or a combination of grains. Because dogs cannot digest fiber, it is used in many dog foods, particularly weight-reduction diets, to maintain dry-matter bulk.

Vitamins are necessary for good health and many of the biochemical reactions that take place in the body. Depending upon how vitamins are absorbed and excreted by the body, they are classified as fat-soluble (vitamins A, D, E, and K) or water-soluble (all the B vitamins and vitamin C). Dogs are capable of making their own vitamin C and do not require vitamin C supplementation in their diet (unlike humans, non-human primates, and guinea pigs, who will develop scurvy and die without dietary vitamin C). Vitamins must be correctly balanced in a dog's diet. Excess vitamin intake, or a vitamin deficiency, can cause serious medical problems.

Minerals include calcium, phosphorus, sodium, potassium, magnesium, zinc, selenium, iron, manganese, copper, iodine, and other chemical elements. Minerals are necessary for skeletal growth and development, muscle and nerve function, and life sustaining biochemical reactions that take place in the body daily. Like vitamins, minerals should be provided in a balanced ratio. Excessive supplementation of minerals can lead to serious medical conditions.

Additives and preservatives are substances added to the dog food to enhance color, flavor, and texture and extend product shelf-life. Antioxidants are added to dog food to help keep fat in the food from becoming rancid over time. Other additives are used to delay bacterial and fungal growth.

Supplements

If you are feeding Willie a high-quality dog food, nutritional supplementation is most likely unnecessary. In fact, by supplementing him with other products, you may disrupt the nutritional balance you are striving to provide. Consult your veterinarian about any form of supplementation you are considering before adding it to Willie's nutritional program.

How Much to Feed

Nutritional needs will vary according to the stage of development, activity level, and environmental conditions. Basic feeding guidelines are provided on the dog food label, but the suggested amount per feeding may be more than Willie requires. Just as you would not eat the same amount of food as your next-door neighbor, no two dogs are alike in their feeding requirements. Although there are all kinds of calculations you can do to determine Willie's energy requirements and caloric intake, they probably will vary weekly, and possibly daily, especially if he is a young, active, growing puppy.

Teach your Fox Terrier manners. Don't allow it to beg for food while you are cooking or eating. If your pet's antics and pleading eyes are too difficult to ignore, keep your companion in the backyard or in another room during family mealtimes.

The amount you feed Willie also will depend on the quality of the food you provide. If you feed a high-quality dog food that is easily digested, a smaller amount will be needed than if you feed a mediocre diet filled with bulk and material that cannot be digested. You also will notice that Willie will produce less fecal material when fed a quality diet, because most of the food is used for energy and less is going to waste.

The best way to know if Willie is eating the proper amount is to check his overall physical condition. *You should be able to feel the ribs, but not see them.* Weigh him once a week, if possible, and not less than once a month. You can do this by holding Willie and weighing both of you on a bathroom scale, then weighing yourself alone. Subtract your weight from the combined weight and the difference will be Willie's weight. Another option is to ask

your veterinarian if you can use the hospital walk-on platform scale each week. If you notice any weight loss or gain, your veterinarian can advise you if Willie is within the appropriate weight range and whether to change the diet or meal size. Remember that an adult Fox Terrier should weigh about 18 pounds (8 kg).

When to Feed

Fox Terrier puppies are active individuals that burn off calories quickly. Their initial growth phase is during the first 6 months of life, although technically they are still puppies until 8 to 12 months of age, or when they reach puberty. While Willie is a puppy, he should be fed at least four times a day because he has a small stomach and a high metabolism. As a general guideline, when his growth and development begin to slow down, you can decrease the feeding schedule to three meals (at about 12 weeks of age), and later two meals (at about 6 months of age) a day. Be sure to consult your veterinarian to be certain this feeding schedule matches Willie's specific needs.

Unless Willie is a hard-working, very active Fox Terrier, he probably will not require more than one to two meals a day when he is an adult. Ideally the meals should be provided at 12-hour intervals, or if only one meal is provided, in the early evening, after he has exercised and before bedtime. If all of the food has not been eaten after 20 minutes, remove it. An after-dinner leisurely stroll before bedtime will help Willie sleep more comfortably.

Some people prefer to feed free choice (also called "free feed" or *ad libitum*), which means that food is available at all times and the dog eats whenever it desires. This method works well for dogs that are nibblers, not gluttons. Although free-choice feeding is convenient, it is difficult to know exactly how much food is eaten daily. It also is not usually successful because most dogs will eat even if they are not hungry. These gourmands eventually will exceed their ideal weight if food is not limited.

Obesity

Obesity is a form of malnutrition in which there is a ratio of too much fat to lean body

Develop Good Eating Habits

✔ Designate a place for the dog food bowl and put everything Willie is to eat in the bowl. This will discourage him from begging food from your hands or from the dinner table.

✔ Feed on a regular schedule.

✔ Do not feed Willie human snack foods and candies. They are high in sugars and salts.

✔ Do not feed meat, fish, poultry, or eggs raw. These products can be contaminated with *Salmonella, E. coli*, or other bacterial pathogens that can cause fatal illness.

✔ Do not feed bones. They can splinter and become lodged in the throat or gastrointestinal tract.

✔ Determine in advance which food treats, and how many, Willie will be allowed each day. Do not exceed the limit you have set.

✔ Feed snacks and treats primarily as training rewards or special praise.

✔ Teach children not to feed meals or give treats to Willie without your permission.

✔ Do not allow Willie in the kitchen while you are preparing food, or in the dining room during family mealtime. This prevents begging.

tissue. We usually think of malnutrition as a deficiency in food rather than excess. However, malnutrition means improper (or bad) nutrition and refers to all aspects of unbalanced nutrition. Obesity in dogs has now reached epidemic proportions in the United States—a staggering 30 percent of the canine population is obese. Overfeeding (especially overfeeding a puppy or adolescent) and inactivity can cause obesity, which in turn can lead to heart disease, skeletal and joint problems (such as arthritis), and metabolic diseases (such as diabetes).

Water

Water is the most important of all nutrients. Water is necessary for life because it is required for digestion, to metabolize energy, and to eliminate waste products from the body. Although you would never deprive Willie of food, he could survive longer without food than without water. A 10 percent body water loss will result in death, and water makes up more than 70 percent of your companion's lean adult body weight.

Dogs lose body water throughout the day, in the urine and feces, by evaporation, panting, drooling, and footpad sweating. Water depletion occurs more rapidly in warm or hot weather, or when an animal is active. Body water must continually be replaced, so it is extremely important that fresh water be available at all times to avoid dehydration and illness.

It is important to monitor how much water Willie drinks each day. If he seems to be continually thirsty or to drink more than usual, it could be a warning sign for possible illness, such as diabetes or kidney disease. If he is not drinking as much as he should, he can become dehydrated and develop a medical condition.

TIP

The Right Dishes

Use stainless steel food dishes. Plastic or hard rubber dishes can cause skin allergies (contact dermatitis) in some animals.

Adequate water intake is especially important in older animals, as they may have impaired kidney function. If you think Willie is drinking too much, or not drinking enough, contact your veterinarian right away.

Food Myths

There are some common food myths about the effects of various foods in the canine diet. Garlic is often credited with killing worms and repelling fleas. Brewer's yeast and onions have also been touted as flea repellants. Unfortunately, these foods have no action against internal or external parasites, although dogs can benefit from the B vitamins in Brewer's yeast. Onions, on the other hand, can cause toxicity in dogs and are not recommended in the diet.

Food Allergies

Just like people, dogs can develop allergies to certain foods. For example, some dogs are sensitive to corn (a major ingredient in many commercial dog foods) or corn oil, or beef in the diet.

Food allergies often express themselves by their effect on the animal's skin and coat. If Willie is scratching his skin excessively, for no apparent reason, and his coat does not look its best, ask your veterinarian if a change to a hypoallergenic diet would be beneficial.

KEEPING YOUR FOX TERRIER HEALTHY AND HAPPY

In earlier times, it was not unusual for dogs to die from a wide variety of health problems, ranging from malnutrition to severe parasitism to deadly bacterial and viral diseases.

The modern-day dog is a lucky dog indeed, benefiting from all the medical advances, prescription products, good nutrition, and creature comforts that people enjoy.

Today's veterinarian has received years of training in medicine and surgery and many veterinary clinics are subject to inspection and accreditation. If Anna requires medical expertise in a specific area, board certified veterinary specialists are available to help.

It is reassuring to know so many resources are available if they are ever needed, but *the best way to keep your pet healthy is to avoid or prevent problems before they start.* Preventive health care is the most important care you can give your dog. It includes regular physical examinations, vaccinations against disease, an

Regular exercise is an important part of your Fox Terrier's preventive health care program.

effective parasite control program, correct nutrition (see Feeding Your Fox Terrier), regular exercise, good dental care, routine grooming (see At Home with Your Fox Terrier), and plenty of love and attention to ensure Anna's physical and emotional well-being.

Selecting a Veterinarian

You and your veterinarian will be partners sharing responsibility for ensuring your companion's health throughout her life. For this reason, you will be as particular about choosing Anna's veterinarian as you are about your own doctor. Fortunately, there is no shortage of excellent veterinarians, but how do you find the veterinarian that's just right for you and Anna? Here are some guidelines to help you in the selection process.

1. Ideally, you will want to find a veterinarian who appreciates Fox Terriers as much as

you do and who is familiar with the breed's special characteristics. Start looking for a veterinarian before you need one.

2. Ask satisfied Fox Terrier owners and members of the local kennel clubs which veterinarians they recommend in your area. Word of mouth is one of the best ways to find a veterinarian. Many veterinarians advertise in telephone directories, but the size or style of an advertisement is not an indicator of the best match for your requirements.

3. Consider convenience. What are the doctors' office hours, schedule, and availability? Who is available on weekends and holidays, or in case of emergency? How close is the veterinary clinic or hospital? Will you be able to travel there within a reasonable amount of time in the event of an emergency?

4. Is there a consistency of personnel and continuity of communication? The veterinary support staff will play an important role in Anna's health care. Have the veterinary technicians (animal health care nurses) received formalized, certified training, and are they licensed?

5. What are the fees for services? Most veterinarians provide a price estimate for anticipated services and expect payment when service is rendered. Be sure to ask what types of payment methods are available.

6. Request an appointment to tour the veterinary hospital facilities. Examine all of the hospital during your tour, particularly as it concerns cleanliness and odors, the surgical suites and isolation wards, and the availability of monitoring equipment for surgery and anesthesia.

You and your veterinarian will develop a relationship of mutual respect and trust. You will rely on each other for accurate information and work together as a team. The chemistry between you, your veterinarian, and Anna should be just right.

Preventive Health Care

Physical Examinations

You know your companion better than anyone. You know when Anna is happy and feeling great, and you will be the first to notice if she is not acting herself, seems depressed, doesn't want to eat, is limping, is losing weight, or has any other problems. Of course, under these circumstances you would call your veterinarian to schedule an appointment for a physical examination, diagnosis, and treatment. However, the more you know about Anna's condition, and the sooner you recognize any potential problems, the more you can help her—and your veterinarian.

A home physical examination is a good way to detect a possible problem before it becomes serious. The home examination is not a replacement for the veterinary examination, but it gives you a good idea of your dog's health condition. If you notice something wrong with Anna, call your veterinarian right away and describe your observations and concerns. Keep a record of Anna's condition, noting the date and the time. Add information to the record if there are any changes. This information will be useful in assessing the progression or improvement of a condition over time.

In order to detect illness in an animal, you must first be able to recognize normal appearance, attitude, stance, movement, and behavior. Here are a few things to look for when you examine your Fox Terrier.

1. First, watch Anna from a distance. Does she have a happy attitude and does she appear to be in good condition? Is her coat healthy? Is she well-proportioned (not too thin, not too heavy)? Do you see anything unusual?

2. Observe Anna while she stands. Does she stand naturally and are her feet correctly placed? Does she place all of her weight on all four feet, or is she favoring one foot, or shifting weight from foot to foot? If she holds her neck outstretched, it may mean she is having difficulty breathing. If her back is hunched up, she may have back or abdominal pain. Are her head and neck held in a natural position, or drooping? A dropped head may mean neck pain. A tilted head could indicate ear pain, ear infection, parasites in the ear, or a nervous system problem.

3. Make Anna sit and observe her position. Does she look relaxed and natural, or does she appear uncomfortable? If she holds her elbows out at her sides it may mean she has difficulty breathing.

4. Now watch Anna's movement and gaits. Does she walk, trot, and run willingly and normally, or does she move with difficulty? If she limps, does she limp in the front or the rear? Does she seem to experience pain, or wince when you handle her feet or legs? Does her head bob when she moves? If her head drops or dips more than usual, especially with every other step, it could indicate lameness. The origin of lameness is often difficult to detect, especially if the dog is lame in more than one limb. Lameness could be due to injury, joint problems, muscular or skeletal problems, or nervous system problems. Sometimes lameness is due to a foreign object, like a thorn in the footpad, or a grass awn lodged between the toes, so be sure to check all four of Anna's feet.

5. Now bring Anna in for the close-up examination, from the nose to the toes. And yes, a cold, wet nose is normal for a dog, although a dry nose does not necessarily mean she is sick. The nose should be free of discharge (thick mucus or pus).

With all her busy digging activities, Anna will get dirt lodged in the little "corner grooves" of her nose (the nares). This is normal and can be gently cleaned away with a soft Kleenex or cotton-tipped swab and warm water. If the nares become sore or raw, ask your veterinarian for some ointment to help protect it while it heals. You can also spread a thin layer of Vaseline or Aquaphor over the area, taking care not to plug the nasal passages. Frequent applications are usually necessary because dogs usually lick off medication on the nose shortly after it is applied.

6. Check Anna's eyes. They should be bright and clear. If the colored part of the eye(s) (the iris) appears hazy or cloudy, this could indicate a problem with the cornea, the lens, or the entire globe of the eye. Corneal injuries can be very painful (especially in bright light) and require immediate veterinary attention. Check Anna's eyes up close. The pupil (the black center) of each eye should match in size and shape. They should both shrink in size in the sunlight and become larger when she is in a dark room. Check the eyelids. Do they fit properly over the eyes, or are they turned inward or outward? Do the eyelashes grow outward, or do they turn inward and rub on the surface of the eye? What about the white part of the eye (the sclera)? Is it clear, or is it red (bloodshot)? Check inside the bottom eyelids. They should be bright pink and free of discharge, debris, or pus. Pale eyelids could mean Anna has a low red blood count and is anemic. If they are bright red, this could be a sign of inflammation. If there is pus inside the bottom eyelid, or in the corner of the eye, Anna may have an infection.

7. Look inside Anna's mouth. Do the teeth fit together properly? Are they free of tartar accumulation, or do they need to be cleaned and

polished? Are the gums bright pink? Some dogs naturally have black pigment on their tongues and gums, but very pale pink, white, or muddy gray colored gums or a bluish tongue indicates serious illness in a Fox Terrier. Does Anna have bad breath? It has been estimated that more than 85 percent of adult dogs suffer from some degree of periodontal disease, and this can cause bad breath. Depending on the odor, some types

---

TIP

Checking Temperature

Normal body temperature for a Fox Terrier ranges from 99.5 to 102.5°F (37.5 to 39°C). An excited dog may have an elevated temperature as high as 103.5°F, but it should not exceed this value. Lubricate the tip of the thermometer with Vaseline or Aquaphor and gently insert it approximately two inches into the rectum. Wait two minutes, or, if you are using a digital thermometer, wait for the beep, then check the temperature reading.

Observe your pet from a distance for an overall assessment of its condition, attitude, posture, and gait.

of bad breath can also indicate a metabolic problem, such as ketosis.

8. Look inside Anna's ears. Does she shake her head or scratch at her ears? Her behavior could mean she has an ear infection or parasites, such as ear mites. It is normal for dogs to produce earwax, but excessive wax production, or very dark to black earwax, or a yellow discharge, requires a professional examination and appropriate medical treatment.

9. Now look at Anna's hair and skin. Is the skin healthy, or is it dry and flaky, or greasy? Is there evidence of parasitism, such as fleas or ticks?

10. Moving on to the chest, you can observe Anna's body conformation as well as her ease in breathing and respiration rate. Can you see her ribs? They should not protrude but you should be able to feel them under a layer of muscle. If you cannot feel her ribs, she is too heavy. Although you may not be able to listen to Anna's heart well through her chest, you can still measure her heart rate. To do this, simply press your fingers against the inside middle portion of her upper thigh. You will feel her pulse. Normal heart rate will range between 80 and 120 beats per minute, depending on whether she is at rest or has just been very active.

11. The abdomen should be tucked up neatly. It should not appear bloated or distended. Check the umbilical area ("belly button") and groin area for hernias. If you notice anything unusual, contact your veterinarian right away.

12. Finally, we come to Anna's "south end." If she has not been spayed, check her regularly for signs of estrus. You don't want to leave her within reach of unwanted suitors during her estrous cycle. If you have an intact male (not neutered), Willie should have both testicles fully descended into the scrotum. If one or both testicles are missing, give your veterinarian a call. Retained testicles may be an inherited problem. If the retained testicle is not surgically removed, it can become cancerous in later life. It is wise to check Willie's genital area periodically because it is not unusual for active dogs to accidentally bump and injure themselves. Finally, check under the tail for signs of problems such as swelling, hernias, anal gland problems, cysts, inflammation, diarrhea, and parasites (tapeworms).

Vaccinations

Vaccinations are the best method currently available to protect Anna against serious, life-threatening diseases. Although you will do your

The type of vaccinations your Fox Terrier receives, as well as the vaccine schedule, are health decisions made on an individual case basis.

Vaccination Schedule for Puppies

Vaccine	Age for first inoculation	Age for second inoculation	Age for third inoculation
Distemper	8 weeks	12 weeks	16 weeks
Hepatitis	8 weeks	12 weeks	16 weeks
Parvovirus	8 weeks	12 weeks	16 weeks*
Parainfluenza	8 weeks	12 weeks	16 weeks
Leptospirosis	12 weeks	16 weeks	
Bordetella	12 weeks	16 weeks	
Lyme Disease**	12 weeks	16 weeks	
Coronavirus***	8 weeks	12 weeks	
Rabies****	12 weeks	15 months	

*Some veterinarians recommend a fourth parvovirus vaccination at 20 weeks of age because some animals do not develop sufficient immunity against this disease before 5 months of age.
**Check with your veterinarian to see if Lyme Disease is a problem in your area or in any areas in which you will be traveling with your pet.
***Coronavirus vaccination may not be necessary. Consult your veterinarian.
****Rabies vaccination intervals vary according to state laws and the type of vaccines used. Consult your veterinarian.

Common Canine Diseases

Disease	Cause	Spread	Contagion
Distemper	Viral	Airborne; body excretions.	Highly contagious, especially among young dogs.
Parvovirus	Viral	Contaminated feces.	Highly contagious, especially among puppies.
Infectious canine hepatitis	Viral	Body excretions; urine.	Highly contagious, especially among puppies and young dogs.
Leptospirosis	Bacterial	Urine contaminated in kennels or from wild animals.	Highly contagious.
Parainfluenza Bordetellosis Both cause "kennel cough"	Viral Bacterial	Airborne; sneeze and cough droplets.	Highly contagious, especially in boarding kennels and dog shows.
Coronavirus	Viral	Feces.	Highly contagious.
Lyme disease	Bacterial	Spread by the bite of an infected tick or contaminated body fluids.	
Rabies	Viral	Saliva (bite wounds).	

best to prevent her from coming into contact with sick animals, at some time your companion will be exposed to disease organisms, whether you know it or not. Anywhere you take her—parks, rest stops, campgrounds, dog shows, obedience classes, or to your veterinarian's office—Anna will be exposed to germs that could cause severe illness and possibly death. Although there is not a vaccine available for every known canine disease, we do have vaccines available for the most common and deadly diseases. No vaccine is 100 percent fail-proof; however, if you are conscientious about Anna's health and vaccination schedule, you can rest assured she has a very good chance of being protected against serious illness.

You may note that veterinarians may recommend different vaccination schedules. This is

Symptoms	Treatment
Respiratory: difficulty breathing; coughing; discharge from nose and eyes. Gastrointestinal: vomiting; diarrhea; dehydration. Nervous: trembling; blindness; paralysis; seizures. Skin: pustules on skin; hard footpads.	None. Supportive therapy only.
Gastrointestinal: diarrhea; dehydration; vomiting. Cardiac: heart problems and heart failure.	None. Supportive therapy only.
Liver: inflammation; jaundice. Eyes: "blue eye" due to inflammation and fluid buildup. Kidney: damage, pain, and internal bleeding.	None. Supportive therapy only.
Kidney: damage and failure. Liver: damage and jaundice. Internal bleeding; anemia.	Antibiotics.
Respiratory: dry, hacking, continual cough of several weeks' duration that may cause permanent damage to airways.	Supportive therapy including antibiotics.
Gastrointestinal: vomiting; diarrhea; dehydration.	None. Supportive therapy only.
Swollen lymph nodes; lethargy; loss of appetite; joint swelling; lameness; can induce heart and kidney disease.	Supportive therapy, including antibiotics.
Fatal, preceded by nervous system signs including paralysis, incoordination, and change in behavior.	None. (Post-exposure treatment does exist for humans.)

because *vaccinations should be a medical decision, not a calendar event.* In other words, the type of vaccination and when it is administered should be appropriate to your Fox Terrier's lifestyle, age, health condition, past medical history, and potential risk of exposure. Another reason vaccine schedules may vary is that most vaccine label recommendations are based on historical precedent. For example, it has been found that by vaccinating large populations of animals annually there has been a decline in disease incidence in the overall canine population. However, it has not yet been scientifically demonstrated that vaccinations must be given every year. In fact, vaccines vary in range of purity, potency, safety, and efficacy. Vaccination is a potent medical procedure with profound impact. There are

Internal Parasites

Type	Mode of transmission to dogs	Mode of transmission to humans	Prevention
Roundworms	Ingestion of eggs in feces of infected animals; transmitted from mother to pup in utero or in the milk.	Accidental ingestion of eggs from contact with infected fecal material.	Parasiticides should be administered to pups as early as 3 weeks of age and should be repeated regularly as necessary.
Hookworms	Ingestion of larvae in feces of infected animals; direct skin contact with larvae.	Direct skin contact with larvae in soil contaminated with feces of infected animals; accidental ingestion of larvae.	Parasiticides.
Whipworms	Contact with feces.	No.	Parasiticides.
Tapeworms	Contact with fleas and feces; ingestion of fleas; eating raw meat (wild rodents).	Yes.	Parasiticides.
Heartworms	Mosquito bite.	No.	Parasiticides.
Protozoa	Contact with feces.	Yes.	Parasiticides.

significant benefits, as well as some risks, associated with any vaccine. Vaccine administration should always take into consideration the animal's risk of exposure (population density), susceptibility or resistance to disease, and overall health (nutrition, parasites, age, special medical conditions).

Does your Fox Terrier walk and run normally? Foreign objects, such as grass awns or clumped snow between the footpads, can cause pain and limping.

External Parasites

Type	Animal health problem	Contagious to humans
Fleas	Allergy to flea saliva; skin irritation and itching; transmission of tapeworms.	Fleas may bite humans. Tapeworms may also be indirectly transmitted to people.
Ticks	Transmission of Lyme disease; skin irritation and infection.	Ticks may bite humans and transmit Lyme disease to them
Sarcoptic mange	Skin lesions and itching; hair loss.	Sarcoptic mange can spread from pets to people by contact.
Demodectic mange	Skin lesions; localized or generalized hair loss.	No.

For these reasons, the vaccination schedule on page 65 should be considered only as a guideline. Your veterinarian will determine Anna's vaccination program depending upon her needs and health at the time of examination.

Adult booster vaccinations should be given as recommended by your veterinarian based on your dog's health and specific requirements.

Parasite Control

Giant strides have been made in recent years regarding parasite control, both internal (roundworms, hookworms, whipworms, tapeworms, and heartworms) and external (fleas, ticks, and mange-causing mites). Many products of the past have been replaced by recent, convenient parasiticides. For example, prevention and treatment of internal parasites, heartworm prevention, and treatment for flea infestation can all be accomplished by giving your dog a single tablet monthly. There is a

An alert expression, clear, bright eyes, a damp nose, and a happy attitude are all signs of a healthy Fox Terrier.

variety of pharmaceuticals available to prevent and treat internal and external parasites on a once-a-month basis. These effective, new products are available only from your veterinarian and require a physical examination, a heartworm test, and fecal examination prior to dispensing.

Internal Parasites

Internal parasites (such as worms and protozoa) can have a serious impact on a dog's health. They can cause diarrhea and, in severe cases,

dehydration and malnutrition. In addition, many internal parasites of dogs are transmitted through contact with feces and can pose a serious health threat to people, especially children. This is why it is important to keep Anna in a clean environment and to teach children to wash their hands before eating or after handling any dog.

Illness

If you have to ask yourself whether you should call your veterinarian, then it's a safe bet that you should. If Anna was looking and acting completely healthy and normal, you wouldn't be asking yourself that question. Better to be safe and contact your veterinarian if you think your pet is having a problem. Treating the condition at its very onset can make all the difference between rapid recovery and prolonged illness.

After conducting a physical examination on your companion, contact your veterinarian to discuss any abnormal or unusual findings. Some abnormal findings may not be an illness in and of themselves (such as loss of appetite or listlessness), but they are good indicators that Anna is experiencing other medical problems that require veterinary attention.

First Aid for Your Fox Terrier

In spite of all your efforts to provide a safe environment for your Fox Terrier, accidents can happen and many are life-threatening. The difference between life and death may depend on how prepared you are in an emergency situation. Be sure to have all your supplies on hand in advance so you do not waste precious time during an emergency trying to find what you need to help her. As soon as possible, assemble a first aid emergency kit for Anna. Set aside a special place for the kit. Keep your veterinarian's daytime and emergency telephone numbers close by the phone and keep an additional copy of emergency telephone numbers in the first aid emergency kit.

Supplies for Your First Aid Emergency Kit

There are some basic supplies and materials you will need for your first aid emergency kit.

=== TIP ===

When to Call the Veterinarian

Contact your veterinarian if Anna is having any of the following problems:
- ✔ Fever
- ✔ Pain
- ✔ Loss of appetite
- ✔ Lethargy
- ✔ Vomiting
- ✔ Diarrhea
- ✔ Coughing
- ✔ Sneezing
- ✔ Wheezing
- ✔ Difficulty breathing
- ✔ Difficulty swallowing
- ✔ Choking
- ✔ Limping
- ✔ Head shaking
- ✔ Trembling
- ✔ Blood in the urine or stools
- ✔ Inability to urinate
- ✔ Inability to have a bowel movement
- ✔ Severe constipation
- ✔ Dehydration
- ✔ Weight loss

These items are available from your veterinarian or local drugstore. You will no doubt think of additional things you will want to include in the kit for when you travel or are away from home. For example, bottled water, balanced electrolyte solution (Pedialyte), medication to prevent car-sickness, tranquilizers, and pain killers (available from your veterinarian) are practical items to keep on hand.

First Aid Emergency Care

The goal of first aid treatment is to give Anna whatever emergency care she requires to save her life or to reduce pain and suffering until you can contact your veterinarian. Before you begin any first aid treatment, the most important thing to remember is to protect yourself from being bitten or injured. An animal that is frightened, has been traumatized, or is in pain will not behave nor-mally and can be unpredictable. The friendliest of animals can and do bite when they are injured, in pain, or frightened. Your pet may not recognize you or may instinctively lash out in self-defense at anyone who approaches it. If someone else is available, you can save time by having the person contact your veterinarian for advice while you begin emergency treatment. You may need assis-tance restraining Anna while you treat her, so be sure the person you ask for assistance is experi-enced in animal handling. *Always muzzle your dog before initiating emergency treatment, for the safety of your pet and everyone involved.*

Bite wounds commonly result from battles with other dogs, cats, or wild animals. Fox Terri-ers generally will not initiate a fight, but when a fight breaks out, their terrier instincts take over and they won't back down. In addition to thor-ough cleansing, bite wounds usually require antibiotic therapy to prevent infection. If the

TIP

Using a Muzzle

If you have not yet purchased a muzzle from the pet store, you can make a muzzle using rolled gauze or a cloth strip about two and one half feet long and one inch wide.

Wrap the gauze over the muzzle, making sure it does not pull on all the hair around the face, and tie it securely under the chin. (This will not affect Anna's ability to breathe.) Take the ends of the gauze and tie them behind the head, on top of the neck. This muzzle will not hurt your pet and will protect you from being bitten. Make sure Anna does not try to remove the muzzle with her front paws.

Before you try to help any injured dog, make sure it is securely muzzled.

wound is a tear, it may need to be sutured. If the injury is a puncture wound, it should be cleaned well with hydrogen peroxide and allowed to remain open and drain. Be sure to consult your veterinarian immediately regarding any bite wound injuries. Antibiotics may be necessary to prevent bacterial infection. In addition, if a stray animal or a wild animal (raccoon, skunk, bat) has bitten Anna, you need to discuss the possible risk of rabies in your area with your veterinarian.

Bleeding can occur from injury, trauma, or serious health problems. The first thing you should do is to apply firm pressure over the wound to stop the bleeding. If you do not have a gauze or clean towel, any readily available, clean, absorbent material can be used as a compress. If a large blood vessel in a limb has been severed, it may be necessary to apply a tourniquet above the cut area. A small percentage of Fox Terriers have blood disorders that cause their blood to clot slower than usual, or to not clot at all. (See Selected Diseases and Conditions in Fox Terriers.) If blood loss is severe, your pet can go into shock and die. Contact your veterinarian immediately.

It is not normal for dogs to have bad breath. If your dog's mouth smells bad, check its teeth and gums for tartar accumulation and inflammation. Bad breath can indicate periodontal disease or other health problems.

Bloat (gastric dilatation) is distension of the stomach caused by the accumulation of trapped gas. It is a very painful condition that is life threatening. Bloat usually occurs after excessive activity following consumption of a large meal. As gases build up, the stomach or intestines can twist and the circulation can be blocked. As the animal becomes more bloated, it has difficulty breathing and the pain becomes more intense. Symptoms of bloat include a distended abdomen, retching motions, panting, restlessness, drooling, sitting with elbows pointed away from the body, and eventually collapse, coma, and death.

Bloat is more common in large, deep-chested breeds, but can occur in other breeds. It is a serious emergency situation that requires immediate, urgent treatment to save the animal from a painful death. If you suspect Anna is suffering from bloat, contact your veterinarian immediately.

Signs of bone fractures include swelling, pain and tenderness, abnormal limb position or movement, limping, and crepitation (crackling sensation when the area is touched). When bones are broken, they may remain under the skin or protrude up through the skin (open fracture).

If Anna breaks a leg and the bone is not exposed, you can make a temporary splint out of a piece of wood or folded newspaper or magazine. First, muzzle your Fox Terrier. Then gently tape the splint to the leg, allowing a six-inch overlap at each end of the break site. Do not wrap the splint to the leg so tightly that the paw swells, and do not wrap tape on the injury. If the bone is exposed, do not try to reposition it or cleanse it. Stop the bleeding and cover the wound with a sterile bandage. Make sure Anna does not contaminate the open fracture by licking it. Contact your veterinarian immediately for advice. Anna should receive veterinary care for

Parasites are easily transmitted between dogs. Make sure all of your pets are checked regularly for parasites and treated as necessary.

the broken bone(s) as soon as possible, and definitely within 24 hours.

Three kinds of burns can harm your Fox Terrier: *thermal burns*—from fire, boiling liquids, appliances; *electrical burns*—from chewing on electrical cords; and *chemical burns*—from a variety of chemicals (such as corrosives, oxidizing agents, desiccants, and poisons).

If Willie is burned, immediately cool the burn by applying a cold, wet cloth or an ice pack to the area. Protect the burned area from the air with an ointment (Neosporin or *Aloe vera*). If he has suffered a chemical burn, immediately flush the burn profusely with water or saline to dilute and rinse the caustic chemical from the area. Do not allow Anna to lick the area or she will burn her mouth and esophagus with the substance. Contact your veterinarian immediately.

Choking occurs when an object (bone, food, toy, rock) becomes trapped, or lodged, in the mouth or throat. In this case, your pet is in immediate danger of accidentally inhaling the foreign object. If the object obstructs the air passageway, Anna will suffocate. If she is choking, you will need a good, clear view of her mouth and throat to see if the offending object can be found and safely removed. Fox Terriers have powerful jaws. It will be difficult to pull Anna's jaws open to look into her mouth. Watch your fingers and be careful not to get bitten. A short wooden dowel, 2 to 3 inches (5-6 cm) in diameter, inserted between the back molars, may serve as a gag to hold the mouth open while you use a flashlight to take a closer look down the throat. If

you see the foreign object, be very careful not to push it further down the throat or into the trachea (windpipe). Remove the object with forceps when possible, to avoid being bitten.

Cuts should be cleansed well and treated properly to prevent infection. Sometimes it is difficult to tell how deep the cut is. Serious cuts may require sutures, so be sure to contact your veterinarian for advice. If the cut is not too deep, wash it with a mild soap and rinse it several times with water. Disinfect the injury with hydrogen peroxide or Betadine solution. (Hydrogen peroxide is especially useful for treating puncture wounds.) Dry the wound well and apply an antibiotic ointment to it. If the cut is in an area that can be bandaged, wrap the area with gauze and an elastic bandage to prevent contamination and infection. Change the bandage daily.

Dystocia is the term used when a pregnant female has difficulty giving birth to her young. Dystocia occurs when the smooth muscles of the uterus become fatigued and weakened and can no longer contract. Dystocia also occurs when the uterus becomes twisted, or when the

First Aid Emergency Kit

Item	Purpose
Hydrogen peroxide 3%	Clean cuts and wounds; induce vomiting
Povidone iodine solution	Clean and disinfect wounds
Triple antibiotic ointment	Topical application to cuts and wounds
Kaopectate	Treat diarrhea
Milk of Magnesia	Treat constipation
Ipecac syrup	Induce vomiting
Saline solution (sterile)	Flush and rinse wounds; can be used as an eyewash

Additional Supplies

Bandage scissors	Q-tips	Muzzle
Small, regular scissors	Roll of gauze bandage	Blanket (to provide warmth
Thermometer	Gauze pads (such as Telfa	or to use as a stretcher)
Tourniquet	no-stick pads)	Paper towels
Tweezers	Elastic bandage (preferably	Exam gloves (vinyl is prefer-
Forceps	waterproof)	able to latex because some
Mouth gag	Activated charcoal (in case	people are allergic to latex)
Cotton balls	of poisoning)	Flashlight

mother's pelvic area is abnormal or too small to allow passage of the fetus. In some cases, dystocia occurs because the fetus is too large or not in an appropriate birth position. (It is normal for puppies to be born either hind feet and rump first, or head first).

Dystocia is a medical emergency that requires veterinary expertise. Medications to stimulate uterine contractions, or surgery, may be required to successfully deliver live pups. For this reason it is a good idea to give your veterinarian advance notice of Anna's delivery due date and make back-up arrangements for emergency care if your veterinarian is unavailable the day she gives birth (whelps).

A good rule of thumb is to not allow Anna to be in hard labor for more than two hours. If she has not whelped a pup within that time period, or if she has stopped labor altogether, she very probably needs help. Contact your veterinarian immediately.

Heatstroke is caused by exposure to high temperature and stress. Confinement in a car is one of the leading causes of heatstroke. On a hot day, a car parked in the shade, with the windows partially open, can still reach temperatures exceeding 120°F (49°C) within a few minutes. Overexertion on a hot day can also cause heatstroke. Dogs that are old or overweight are especially prone to heatstroke.

Signs of heatstroke include rapid breathing, panting, bright red gums, vomiting, diarrhea, dehydration, and a rectal temperature of 105 to 110°F (41 to 43°C). As the condition progresses, the body organs become affected, the animal weakens, goes into shock, then a coma, and dies. All of this can happen in a very short period of time and death can occur rapidly.

If Anna is suffering from heatstroke, the first thing you must do is lower her body temperature. You can do this by placing her in a tub filled with cold water. Be sure to keep Anna's head above the water, especially if she is unconscious, so that she does not drown. Do not try to give Anna water to drink if she is unconscious. If a tub is unavailable, you can cool your pet by hosing her with a garden hose or applying ice packs to her body.

Heatstroke is a medical emergency that requires veterinary care. Anna will need to be treated with intravenous fluids and various medications to treat shock and prevent cerebral edema (brain swelling). Contact your veterinarian immediately.

Eye injuries are extremely painful. The sooner you obtain treatment for Anna's eyes, the sooner you can relieve your companion's pain and increase the chances of saving her eyes and vision. Injured eyes are very sensitive to the light, and exposure to even subdued lighting can hurt the eyes. If Anna's injury is such that it requires flushing and rinsing the eye, you can do this using a commercial eyewash solution or saline solution intended for use in the eyes. Place Anna in a dark place and contact your veterinarian immediately. When you transport her to the hospital, place her in a travel crate and cover the crate with a blanket to keep out as much light as possible.

Insect stings can be painful. If a bee stings Anna, remove the stinger with tweezers. (Wasps and hornets do not leave their stingers.) Try to gently remove the stinger without squeezing the base (where part of the bee's body is attached) so that additional venom is not injected into the site. This can be tricky, as the bee's stinger is barbed and the more you push on it, the deeper it penetrates.

Apply baking soda or an ice pack to the area to relieve pain. You may also put a topical antihistamine cream around the stung area. Watch Anna closely for the next two hours for signs of illness.

Most cases of bee, hornet, and wasp stings are painful annoyances; however, some animals develop a hypersensitivity to insect stings that can lead to anaphylactic shock and death. If the swelling worsens, or if Anna becomes restless and has difficulty breathing, or starts to vomit, develops diarrhea, or loses consciousness, then contact your veterinarian immediately. This is a life-threatening situation and immediate professional treatment is necessary.

Poisoning can occur in several ways. In addition to insect venom poisons, pets can be poisoned by eating or inhaling toxic substances, or by contact with poisons on their skin, mucous membranes, or eyes.

Signs of poisoning include restlessness, drooling, abdominal pain, vomiting, diarrhea, unconsciousness, seizures, shock, and death. Common sources of poison include rodent bait, house plants, insecticides, medication overdose, spoiled food, antifreeze (ethylene glycol), and chocolate. (Chocolate contains theobromine, a substance similar to caffeine, that is toxic to dogs.)

If you know the source of Anna's poisoning, contact your veterinarian immediately for advice. If the poison came in a container (for example, antifreeze or rodent poison), read the container label and follow the emergency instructions for treating poisoning. If the

Care Essentials for Older Pets

There are a number of things you can do to keep Anna comfortable in her golden years.

1. Provide a soft, warm bed. Cold temperatures and hard surfaces make arthritis more painful.

2. Weigh Anna monthly and do not allow her to become over- or underweight.

3. Take Anna out regularly for easy, short walks on level, soft, nonslippery surfaces (such as grass). Keep her toenails trimmed.

4. Do not make Anna climb stairs or hills, jump in and out of cars, or walk on slippery surfaces.

5. Feed Anna a diet appropriate for her age and health condition. Old dogs have an increase in protein requirement. An increase in protein quality and quantity has recently been demonstrated to be beneficial for some geriatric dogs, as well as having anti-cancer and antidiabetes effects.

6. Schedule physical examinations for Anna every six months in her geriatric years. This way, you can detect and address any age-related problems (such as cataracts, heart or kidney insufficiency) early. Remember that older dogs are more sensitive to anesthesia, especially if they are overweight.

7. If Anna has failing eyesight or is hard of hearing, make every effort not to startle her. Speak to her reassuringly as you approach so she knows you are there.

instructions state to induce vomiting, you may accomplish this by administering $1/2$ ml per pound of body weight syrup of ipecac or $1/2$ teaspoon of hydrogen peroxide, 3 percent for every ten pounds of body weight.

Activated charcoal is a good compound to use to dilute and adsorb ingested poisons. You can obtain activated charcoal in powder or tablet form from your veterinarian to keep in your first aid kit. If you do not have activated charcoal, and you do not have any products to induce vomiting, you can dilute the poison in the gastrointestinal tract by giving Anna some milk. Do not try to give her any medication if she is unconscious.

The sooner the poisoning is diagnosed and treated, the better Anna's chances of full recovery. Most poisonings require veterinary treatment in addition to the initial emergency care you provide. Contact your veterinarian immediately if you suspect Anna has been exposed to poison.

Porcupine quills: Fox Terriers are determined, tenacious hunters. If you live in the country, at some time your companion will likely encounter a porcupine. These large rodents sport some very impressive, barbed quills that serve as an excellent form of defense. Sharp barbs enable the quills to migrate deep into the tissues, causing pain and infection, until they are so deeply embedded that they can be difficult to find.

If Anna has had an encounter with a porcupine, check first to make sure her eyes have not been injured. If a quill has penetrated her eye(s), call your veterinarian immediately. Almost all porcupine quills are found in the face, mouth, tongue, cheeks, chest, and front legs.

Muzzle Anna and remove the quills as soon as possible so they do not migrate deep into the body tissues. Gently remove the quills with a pair of pliers or forceps. Pull straight out so that you do not bend or break the quills. Disinfect the external areas with hydrogen peroxide or Betadine solution. Check the inside of the mouth, cheeks, tongue, and gums thoroughly for quills. Contact your veterinarian.

Skunk spray: At some time or another during an outing, Anna may discover a skunk. Skunks are small, reclusive, shy, nocturnal animals closely related to minks, ferrets, badgers, and otters. Skunks have two methods of self-defense: warning coloration in the form of an unusual black coat with broad white strips or white spots, making them easy to recognize and avoid, and anal glands that can accurately spray a potent, bright yellow musk with an offensive odor. In the face of danger, a skunk will try to escape, but if cornered or harassed it will threaten with handstands and foot stomping and end the performance by spraying its attacker. Skunk spray will sting the skin and eyes and has been reported in some cases to cause brief, transient blindness. These effects are temporary and Anna will be all right. If she has been sprayed in the eyes, rinse the eyes profusely with a mild eyewash. Several minutes of soft spray from a water hose, followed by some soothing ophthalmic solution is also a good way to rinse skunk spray from the eyes. You can purchase a shampoo specially formulated to neutralize skunk odor (such as Skunk-Off) from your veterinarian or local pet store. Most Fox Terriers learn their lesson after the first skunk encounter, recognizing the skunk's warning coloration. Other Fox Terriers never give up the hunt and are repeatedly sprayed.

Seizures have many causes including epilepsy, poisoning, and brain trauma. Seizures may be mild or severe, ranging from a mild tremor of short duration, to violent convulsions, chomping jaws and frothing at the mouth, stiffening of the neck and limbs, and cessation of breathing. During a severe seizure, a dog is not conscious and can be hurt thrashing about on the floor. Anna

TIP

Home Recipe for Eliminating Skunk Odor

Mix together:
- ✔ 1 quart of 3 percent hydrogen peroxide
- ✔ ¹/₄ cup of baking soda
- ✔ 1 teaspoon of liquid soap

Bathe the dog with the solution. Do not allow the mixture to come into contact with your pet's eyes. Rinse thoroughly with tap water.

The soap acts to break up the oils in the skunk spray, allowing the other ingredients to neutralize the thiols that cause the odor.

Never leave your Fox Terriers in a parked car on a warm day. Temperatures inside the car can soar in a short time period and your pets can rapidly die of heatstroke. Play it safe and take them with you on a leash.

may seem to be choking during a seizure, but avoid the temptation to handle her mouth, as you will be bitten. If her jaws clamp down on your fingers, the jaws will not release until the seizure has ended. Simply try to prevent Anna from injuring herself or hitting her head until the seizure has ended. After a seizure, Anna will be exhausted and seem dazed. Place her in a quiet room with subdued light. Keep her comfortable and warm, and when she is conscious offer her some water to drink. Contact your veterinarian immediately for follow-up medical care to determine the cause of the seizure and how to prevent another one from occurring.

Shock is a condition in which there is a decreased blood supply to vital organs and the body tissues die from inadequate energy production. Blood loss, heatstroke, bacterial toxins, and severe allergic reactions can all cause an animal to go into shock.

Shock is a serious emergency situation that results in a rapid death unless immediate veterinary care, including fluid and oxygen therapy and a variety of medications, is available. Signs of shock include vomiting, diarrhea, weakness, difficulty breathing, increased heart rate, collapse, and coma.

Snakes, Toads, Lizards, and Spiders

Because your Fox Terrier is an adventurer who doesn't miss a thing, it is important to be aware of additional risks she may encounter away from home, particularly on camping trips.

Poisonous Snakebites

There are three groups of venomous snakes in North America: the pit vipers, which include the rattlesnake, copperhead, and water mocassin (also known as the cottonmouth); the coral snakes; and the colubrids. The pit vipers and coral snakes are the most dangerous. Rattlesnake bites occur most frequently in dogs, particularly in the west and southwest where rattlesnakes are common. The snake's bite will produce painful, slit-like, puncture wounds that rapidly become swollen. Common symptoms of snakebite include immediate severe pain, swelling, darkened tissue coloration, and tissue necrosis (tissue death).

Urgent, immediate veterinary attention is necessary. The lethality of the snakebite depends upon the type of venom and its toxicity, the amount of venom injected, the size and health of the bitten victim, and the amount of time that passes from the time of the bite until medical care is provided. Poisonous snakebites require antivenin and antibiotic treatments. If the bite is left untreated, the skin and underlying tissue may turn dark and slough off (rot). However, the amount of venom injected (envenomation) cannot be determined simply by the appearance of the bite wound. The bite victim may become weak and exhibit various neurological signs, such as respiratory depression, and eventually go into shock and die.

If a venomous snake bites Anna, contact your veterinarian immediately. Most veterinarians who practice in areas where snakebites are common keep antivenin available. All dogs bitten by venomous snakes should be hospitalized and monitored for at least 24 hours.

Toad Poisoning

Poisonous toads in the United States include the Colorado Rim Toad and the Marine Toad. The most toxic toad varieties are located in the southwestern desert and southeastern United States and Hawaii. If you suspect Anna has come in contact with a poisonous toad, contact a veterinarian immediately for specific treatment recommendations.

Lizard Bites

The poisonous Gila Monster lizard is found in the southwestern United States. It has grooved teeth (instead of fangs) with which it holds onto its victims. Most dogs are bitten on the upper lip. The Gila Monster bite is extremely painful. No antivenin is available. Contact your veterinarian immediately for supportive treatment, antibiotics, and treatment to prevent shock.

Spiders

The brown spiders (Fiddleback, Brown Recluse, and Arizona Brown Spider) are all found in the southern United States. There is no antidote available for their venomous bites. black widow spiders are found throughout the United States. There is an antivenin available for black widow bites.

If Anna is bitten by one of these spiders, take her to a veterinarian immediately for emergency care, antibiotic therapy, and antivenin therapy (for black widow spider bite).

The Senior Fox Terrier

With tender loving care, good nutrition, and a little luck, your Fox Terrier may live for 12 to 16 years or more. Just like people, some dogs age more slowly than others, especially those that have received good health care throughout their lives. As a general rule, a Fox Terrier is not quite a senior citizen until it reaches seven years of age. Fox Terriers are stoic and keenly alert, so it may

not be easy to see some of the first signs of age, such as joint pain, poor vision, hearing loss, and a greater reliance upon sense of smell. As Anna's body ages, it undergoes a slowing of metabolic rate that can lead to weight gain; a weaker heart and a reduction in kidney and liver function; tooth loss and periodontal disease; cataracts; joint degeneration, skin and hair problems; general muscle weakening and atrophy; and a gradual deterioration in condition with a decreased resistance to diseases. Anna may even show signs of disorientation or senility. All of these age-related changes, and the rate at which they occur, vary between individuals and are influenced by genetics, nutrition, environment, and the type of health care received in earlier years.

Euthanasia—When It's Time to Say Good-bye

Euthanasia means putting an animal to death humanely, peacefully, and painlessly. There are different ways veterinarians euthanize animals, depending on the circumstances. Euthanasia is usually done by first giving the animal a sedative to make it sleep deeply and then giving it a lethal substance by injection that ends its life almost instantly.

Even with the best care in the world, the sad day will come when you must consider euthanasia for your beloved companion. Understandably, this will be an emotionally painful time for you, because you will feel helpless in your inability to help your friend anymore, you will not want her to suffer for a moment, yet you will not be able to bear the thought of life without her. Nevertheless, if you begin to ask yourself whether your pet should be euthanized, there must be good

As your Fox Terrier ages, try to be more sensitive to its needs. An older dog may suffer from arthritis, hearing loss, and failing eyesight. There are many ways you can keep your senior friend comfortable and content in the golden years.

reasons. The decision of when to euthanize is a difficult one that depends upon many things. A good rule of thumb is, if suffering cannot be relieved, or if the quality of life is poor, or if the "bad days" simply outnumber the "good days," it is time to discuss euthanasia with your veterinarian. Your veterinarian can answer any specific questions you or your family may have. Your veterinarian can also help you if you wish to find a pet cemetery or desire cremation services.

During this emotional time, remember to take care of yourself and allow time to grieve. If you have children in the family, deal with the issue of animal loss at a level they can understand, comfort them, and let them share their grief. (See Children and Fox Terriers). Take comfort in the knowledge that you took excellent care of your Fox Terrier throughout her life and that you made the best decisions regarding her health and welfare, even when you had to make the most difficult decision of all.

Selected Diseases and Conditions in Fox Terriers

Fox Terriers are strong, sturdy, resilient dogs. Throughout the century they have been recognized for their hardiness and stamina. But like every other breed of dog, or animal species, Fox Terriers can have problems. Each breed of dog is predisposed to various conditions or disorders. This does not mean that the problems are unique to a specific breed. Many dog breeds share the same health problems. It also doesn't mean your dog will ever experience any of these problems, or that the problem is widespread within the breed. It simply means that when there are problems, these are the types most commonly observed in the breed. So don't let this list of problems frighten you. Most likely, Anna will not have any of these conditions, but if she does, this list will help you recognize the problem at the onset.

1. Dental: abnormal placement or number of teeth

2. Eyes: lens luxation, inverted eyelids (entropion), glaucoma

3. Bone and joint: inflammation of the joint cartilage (osteochondritis dessicans), abnormal formation of the joint cartilage (osteochondrosis), shrinking of blood vessels supplying nutrients to the head of the femur (Legg-Perthe Disease)

4. Skin: allergies

5. Hearing: deafness

6. Heart: pulmonic stenosis, Tetralogy of Fallot

7. Thyroid: hypothyroidism

8. Blood clotting: von Willebrand's Disease

Training Essentials

Good health and good manners are both essential to a totally enjoyable companion. When Willie feels his best, he will probably do his best. This is as important for everyone he will meet as it is for those in his immediate family circle.

In order to be an acceptable member of society, Willie will need to learn some basic manners. Because Fox Terriers are extremely bright and eager to please, basic training is easy. But don't forget that Fox Terriers are easily excited, so don't let Willie get distracted. He will astound you with how quickly he learns his lessons, as long as he stays focused. The best way to keep Willie's attention is to keep training sessions short, make them fun and interesting, and always end on a positive note.

Training a Fox Terrier begins the moment you bring one home. It is never too early to

Fox Terriers are generally hardy, healthy dogs.

start with simple, basic lessons. Studies have shown, for example, that leash-training is easiest when a puppy is anywhere from five to nine weeks of age.

Fox Terriers radiate confidence and adapt readily to unusual situations. Studies have shown that Fox Terriers scored very high in tests that called for confidence in strange situations; however, they did poorly in maze tests when they became overexcited and made many mistakes.

A basic puppy class, or dog training class, is the most effective way to begin obedience training and teach Willie to pay attention. There are as many different training techniques as there are dogs and trainers.

Dog training classes are a lot of fun. They are rewarding not only because your canine becomes a model citizen, but because you will also form many long-lasting friendships. Here are some training guidelines to get you started.

HOW–TO: BASIC TRAINING

Come

Willie must first learn his name so he can come when he is called and later respond to your commands. Start by calling his name when you feed him. It won't take him long to associate his name with a pleasant experience. In the beginning, you may also use small tidbits as a reward, along with much praise, when Willie comes to you. Don't show him that you have a food reward. Keep him guessing. Over time, decrease the frequency of food rewards but continue the praise. In no time at all, Willie will come to you when called, purely for the attention you bestow on him, but that doesn't mean you still can't occasionally surprise him with a very small food reward!

Sit

Teach Willie to sit by holding a small piece of food over his nose and raising your hand over his head. As his head goes up to follow the tidbit, his hindquarters will naturally go down, and you may apply gentle pressure on the rump to help him sit in the beginning. Give Willie a tidbit reward as soon as he is seated. As training progresses you may wait longer intervals before giving him the tidbit and eventually replace the food reward with praise.

Down

Teach Willie to lie down by starting him in a sitting position. Kneel down alongside of him, on his right-hand side, facing the same direction, and rest your hand lightly on his shoulders. Show Willie a food reward and then slowly lower the food to the ground in front of him. This should encourage him to lie down to reach the food, but in the beginning you may have to apply light pressure to the top of his shoulders or pull one leg gently out in front of him. Once Willie is in the down position, praise him and give him a food reward. As with other commands, you will eventually replace the food reward with praise alone.

Leash–training

After you have trained Willie to come when called and to follow you around the yard, you are ready to begin leash-training. Begin by attaching a light line, such as string or yarn, to his collar and allow him to drag the line

As you raise the food reward above your pet's nose, his rump will drop down and he will naturally go into a "sit" position.

behind him and to play with it. Encourage him to follow you with the string dangling along. When he has become accustomed to the string, replace it with the leash. Willie will quickly adapt to the leash dragging on the ground, and when he has you can then pick it up and walk with him. Begin by holding the leash and following Willie wherever he goes. This way he will not fight the leash or consider it a threat. He will probably ignore it.

As your training sessions progress, you will begin to guide your pet. Decide where you want to go, and with Willie on the leash, encourage him with words and praise to follow you to that location. In the beginning the distance should be short, maybe just halfway across the backyard. If Willie elects not to come along, simply stop where you are and wait. Don't drag him or pull on him. He may struggle against the leash at first, trying to get away, but he will quickly learn that any pulling or discomfort is created by his own activities and there is no resistance if he follows you. As soon as Willie gives up the fight and approaches you or follows you, praise him for his common sense and end the training session

Some gentle pressure over the shoulders will teach your Fox Terrier to remain in the "down" position.

shortly thereafter on a positive note with a food reward.

With patience, praise, and consistency in training, Willie will be following along on the leash in no time. He may weave a bit, or run a little ahead, or drop behind for a moment to investigate something interesting on the ground, but he will now have the general idea. Once he reaches this level in his leash-training, you can begin to work on fine-tuning him to heel.

THE VERSATILE FOX TERRIER

Fox Terriers are not only balanced and beautiful, they are quick, agile, and coordinated. They are also highly intelligent and full of energy. There is no limit to the things they can learn and do. So let's take a look at some of the fun ways you can put Willie's talents to the test!

Earthdog Tests

Fox Terriers were bred and raised to hunt vermin and "go to earth" after them in their dens and burrows. One way to show off your companion's natural abilities and instincts is by participating in earthdog tests. Dogs may earn titles in three levels of American Kennel Club Earthdog Tests: Junior Earthdog, Senior Earthdog, and Master Earthdog.

Junior Earthdog is a basic instinct test. The dog must travel through a 30-foot-long underground tunnel with three 90 degree turns. At the end of the tunnel is the prey (usually rats in protective caging). When the dog discovers the prey it is expected to bark and dig and pull at the cage with its mouth and paws. The "work" should continue for 60 seconds.

At the Senior Earthdog level, the test becomes more like a real hunt. The entrance to the tunnel is hidden so the dog must use its sense of smell to find it. There is also a false entrance and a false den with no prey. If the

Fox Terriers are arguably the most clever, animated, and versatile of all dog breeds.

dog enters the false den, called a "dead hole," it is disqualified. When the dog finds the live prey at the end of the tunnel, it must "work" for a minimum of 90 seconds.

Master Earthdog tests most closely mirror a real hunt. Dogs work in braces of two and are released 100 feet from the den. The first dog to find the entrance is the first to enter and work. After the first dog has completed working, the second dog is allowed to go inside and work. While one dog is inside the den working, its partner is staked outside and must remain quiet, or "honor" the working dog.

In order to earn the Junior Earthdog title, a dog must have two qualifying legs. Three qualifying legs are required for the Senior Earthdog title, and four for the Master Earthdog title. An Earthdog Test rule book may be obtained from the American Kennel Club.

Dog Shows

Dog shows are a lot of fun for both exhibitors and observers. Dogs are judged on how closely they come to the ideal standard for conformation for their breeds. If Willie is handsome enough to compete against the best of his breed, consider joining a Fox Terrier club, as well as a local kennel club. These clubs can provide you with information on show dates and locations, judges, professional handlers, canine activities, and even offer handling classes to teach you and your dog the ropes. Dog clubs also organize fun matches—dog shows where you can practice and perfect what you've learned before you participate in an all-breed or specialty (one breed only, in your case, Fox Terriers) show.

Fun Matches

You can prepare yourself and your puppy for a future in the conformation ring by attending fun matches. Fun matches are just that— fun! They are hosted by American Kennel Club–approved breed clubs and conducted according to American Kennel Club show rules. Only purebred, AKC-registered dogs may participate. However, fun matches do not count toward points for a championship and dogs that have won points toward a championship do not compete. Judges at fun matches may be official AKC judges, or knowledgeable dog

breeders or handlers selected by the hosting club. Fun matches are a great way for you and your puppy to practice all aspects of a real dog show, from traveling to grooming to exhibiting to winning!

Specialty Shows

Under American Kennel Club show rules, there are three types of conformation shows: specialty shows, group shows, and all-breed shows. Dogs are judged against their breed standard and, by a process of elimination, one dog is selected Best of Breed.

A specialty show is limited to one breed; for example, the American Fox Terrier Club holds an annual show for Fox Terriers only. A group show offers classes for all the breeds in one AKC group. An all-breed show offers classes for every breed.

The American Fox Terrier Club is responsible for maintaining the official standards of the breed. If there are any changes or revisions to be made, the club must approve it before submitting it for final approval to the AKC.

In order to become a champion, a Fox Terrier must win a minimum of 15 points by competing in formal, American Kennel Club–sanctioned, licensed events. The points must be accumulated as major wins under different judges.

Fox Terriers tackle the demanding Agility exercises with the same enthusiasm they radiate in life. Here a Smooth prepares to dive into the Agility tunnel.

All-Breed Shows

As the name implies, all-breed shows are for all breeds. Judging is conducted according to AKC rules. In addition to Best of Breed winners, open shows offer the title of Best in Group (for dogs considered to be the best representative of their group) and Best in Show (for the dog selected as the best representative of its breed and group, compared to all other dogs of other breeds and groups).

Most dogs being shown are competing for points toward their championship. A dog can earn from one to five points at a show. The number of points available depends upon the number of entries. Wins of three, four, or five points are called "majors." The 15 points required for a championship title must be won under at least three different judges and include two majors won under two different judges.

There are six different classes from which a dog can compete for championship points and the classes are divided by sex:

✔ Puppy (divided into 6-9 months of age and 9-12 months of age)
✔ 12–18 Months
✔ Novice
✔ Bred by Exhibitor
✔ American-Bred
✔ Open

Male dogs are judged first in the above order. The first-place winners in each class return to the show ring to compete against each other in what is called the Winners Class. The dog selected as the best male in the Winners Class is the Winners Dog. This is the dog that will win the championship points in the show. The male that placed second to the Winners Dog in his original class (that is, Puppy, 12-18 Months, Novice, Bred by Exhibitor, American-Bred, or Open) is then brought in to join the Winners Class and compete against the remaining dogs in the class. The dog that wins second place in the Winners Class is the Reserve Winners Dog. If, for any reason, the AKC disallows the championship points to the Winners Dog, the Reserve Winners Dog will receive the points. The same procedure is then followed, in the same order, for the females, and the Winners Bitch (who also wins championship points) and Reserve Winners Bitch are selected.

The Winners Dog and Winners Bitch then join a class called the Best of Breed. In this class are entered dogs and bitches that have already won their championship titles. The judge selects one animal to be Best of Breed and either the Winners Dog or the Winners Bitch to be Best of Winners. Finally the judge selects one animal as Best of Opposite Sex to Best of Breed. If the Best of Breed winner is a male, a bitch is Best of Opposite Sex. If the Best of Breed winner is a female, a male is made Best of Opposite Sex.

At an all-breed show, judging takes place for each breed, then each Best of Breed winner competes in its breed group. The seven breed groups are:

✔ Sporting
✔ Hound
✔ Working
✔ Terrier
✔ Toy
✔ Non-Sporting
✔ Herding

The first-place winners of each breed group then compete against each other for the coveted title of Best in Show.

Dog shows are a wonderful way to show off your dog. Here a Smooth Fox Terrier (fourth from left) and a Wire Fox Terrier (sixth from left) compete with other terriers for a placement in Group competition.

Everywhere they go—Fox Terriers love to show off their agility and talents.

A Fox Terrier's enthusiasm is contagious when it gets into a game-playing mode. This sporty canine puts its heart into everything it does!

You should be able to feel your dog's ribs, but not see them. If you can see the ribs, your pet is too thin. If you can't feel the ribs, then your pet is overweight.

Flowers smell nice, but look out for bees! Some dogs develop severe allergies to insect stings.

Fox Terriers make excellent use of their athletic talents.

Obedience Trials

In these competitions, it's intelligence that counts. Dogs are put through a series of exercises and commands and judged according to how well they perform. Each dog starts out with 200 points. Points are deducted throughout the trials for lack of attention, nonperformance, barking, or slowness.

Obedience trials are divided into three levels increasing in difficulty: Novice—Companion Dog (C.D.); Open—Companion Dog Excellent (C.D.X.); and Utility—Utility Dog (U.D.).

To earn a C.D. title, the dog must be able to perform six exercises: heel on leash, stand for examination, heel free, recall, long sit, and long down. To earn a C.D.X. title, the dog must be able to heel free, drop on recall, retrieve on flat, retrieve over the high jump, broad jump, long sit, and long down. To earn a U.D., the dog must be able to respond to signal exercise, scent discrimination tests, directed retrieve, directed jumping, and group examination. The dog must earn three legs to earn its title. To receive a leg

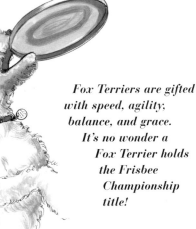

Fox Terriers are gifted with speed, agility, balance, and grace. It's no wonder a Fox Terrier holds the Frisbee Championship title!

the dog must earn at least 170 points out of a possible perfect score of 200 and receive more than 50 percent on each exercise.

Agility Competitions

Agility competitions are lots of fun and extremely popular. They are also competitions at which Fox Terriers can excel. They are fast-paced, challenging events in which dogs compete in obstacle courses, jump over objects, teeter on seesaws, cross bridges, run through tunnels, and weave through poles. The events are timed and are very exciting. Titles that can be earned, in increasing level of difficulty, are: Novice Agility (NA), Open Agility (OA), Agility Excellent (AX), and Master Agility Excellent (MX).

Games

Fox Terriers enjoy all kinds of games, from hide-and-seek, to Flyball, to fetch, to Frisbee. The Fox Terrier is a natural athlete, skilled at games that require stamina, coordination, and agility. It is no wonder that a Fox Terrier holds the title as one of the highest-scoring Freestyle Small Dog Frisbee Champions in the country!

There is no limit to the games and activities a Fox Terrier is capable of learning when given the opportunity. Beautiful, balanced, good-natured, versatile, and full of fun, your Fox Terrier has unlimited potential and will try his best to please you.

No single breed can claim as many successes as the Fox Terrier—the breed that holds the greatest numbers of Best in Show wins at Westminster, the breed that holds the Frisbee Championship title, the breed that can do virtually anything from hunting to guarding to playing games, and do it extraordinarily well—the Fox Terrier is the ultimate canine.

Kennel and Breed Clubs
American Fox Terrier Club
Martin Goldstein, Secretary
P.O. Box 1448
Edison, NJ 08818-1448
e-mail: *mggfc@aol.com*

American Fox Terrier Club
Breeder Referral Information:
Billie Lou Robison
17522 N.E. 195th Street
Woodinville, WA 98072
(425) 483-6177
e-mail: *raybillfox@aol.com*

American Fox Terrier Club Rescue
Winnie Stout
166A Old Plainfield Pike
Foster, RI 02825
(800) FOX-TERR
e-mail: *wstout@edgenet.net*

American Kennel Club (AKC)
Registrations
5580 Centerview Drive
Raleigh, NC 27606-3390
(919) 233-9767
Web site: *www.akc.org*

The Canadian Kennel Club
89 Skyway Avenue, Suite 100
Etobicoke, Ontario, Canada
M9W 6R4
(416) 675-5511

Federation Cynologique Internationale
Secretariat General de la FCA
Place Albert 1er, 13
B-6530 Thuin, Belgium
Web site: *www.fci.be/english*

The Kennel Club
1-4 Clargis Street, Picadilly
London W7Y 8AB England

States Kennel Club
1007 W. Pine Street
Hattieburg, MS 39401
(601) 583-8345

United Kennel Club (UKC)
100 East Kilgore Road
Kalamazoo, MI 49001-5598
(616) 343-9020

United States Dog Agility Association
P.O. Box 850955
Richardson, TX 75085-8955
Tel: (972) 231-9700
Fax: (214) 503-0161
Web site: *www.usdaa.com*
e-mail: *info@usdaa.com*

Health-Related Associations and Foundations
American Society for the Prevention of Cruelty
    to Animals (ASPCA)
424 East 92nd Street
New York, NY 10128-6804
(212) 876-7700
Web site: *www.aspca.org*

American Veterinary Medical Association
(AVMA)
930 North Meacham Road
Schaumberg, IL 60173
Web site: *www.avma.org*

Canine Eye Registration Foundation (CERF)
South Campus Court, Building C
West Lafayette, IN 47907

Training your Fox Terrier begins the moment you bring it home and continues throughout its lifetime.

National Animal Poison Control Center (NAPCC)
Animal Product Safety Service
1717 South Philo Road, Suite 36
Urbana, IL 61802
(888) 4ANI-HELP
(888) 426-4435
(900) 680-0000
(Consultation fees apply; call for details.)
Web site: *www.napcc.aspca.org*

Orthopedic Foundation for Animals (OFA)
2300 Nifong Boulevard
Columbia, MO 65201
Web site: *www.prodogs.com*

Therapy Dogs International
P.O. Box 2796
Cheyenne, WY 82203

Lost Pet Registries
The American Kennel Club (AKC)
AKC Companion Recovery
5580 Centerview Drive, Suite 250
Raleigh, NC 27606-3394
(800) 252-7894
Web site: *www.akc.org/car.htm*
e-mail: *found@akc.org*

Home Again Microchip Service
(800) LONELY-ONE

National Dog Registry (NDR)
P.O. Box 118
Woodstock, NY 12498-0116
(800) 637-3647

Petfinders
368 High Street
Athol, NY 12810
(800) 223-4747

Tattoo-A-Pet
1625 Emmons Avenue
Brooklyn, NY 11235
(800) TATTOOS

Periodicals
The American Kennel Club Gazette
51 Madison Avenue
New York, NY 10010

Dog Fancy
Subscription Division
P.O. Box 53264
Boulder, CO 80323-3264
(303) 786-7306/666-8504
Web site: *www.dogfancy.com*

Dogs USA Annual
P.O. Box 55811
Boulder, Co 80322-5811
(303) 786-7652

Dog World
29 North Whacker Drive
Chicago, IL 60606
(312) 726-2802

Books

The Complete Dog Book, Official Publication of the American Kennel Club. Howell Book House, New York, 1992.

Beak, Linda G. *Wire Fox Terriers*. W. & G. Foyle, Ltd., London, 1960.

Chads, Diana. *The Fox Terrier*. Kingdom Books, London, 1996.

Haynes, Williams. *The Fox Terrier*. MacMillan Company, New York, 1920.

Lee, Rawdon. *The History and Description of Reminiscences of the Fox Terrier*. N.p., 1889.

Nedell, Howard. *The New Fox Terrier*. Howell Book House, New York, 1987.

Pardoe, J. H. *Fox Terriers*. Williams and Norgate, Ltd., London, 1949.

Skelly, George Frank. *All About Fox Terriers*. Orange Judd Publishing Co., Inc., New York, 1948.

Videos

"The Smooth Fox Terrier" (#VVT225)
American Kennel Club Video Fulfillment Department
5580 Centerview Drive, Suite 200
Raleigh, NC 27606
(919) 233-7118

Physical prowess, athletic abilities, and a passion for playing games, perfectly describes the Fox Terrier.

About the Author

Sharon Vanderlip, D.V.M., has provided veterinary care to domestic and exotic animal species for more than 20 years. She has written books and published articles in scientific and lay publications. Dr. Vanderlip has served as the Associate Director of Veterinary Services for the University of California at San Diego School of Medicine; has worked on collaborative projects with the Zoological Society of San Diego; has owned her own veterinary practice; is former Chief of Veterinary Services for the National Aeronautics and Space Administration (NASA), and is a consultant in reproductive medicine and surgery for various research and wildlife projects, including the Endangered Red Wolf project. Dr. Vanderlip has lectured at kennel clubs and veterinary associations throughout America and Europe on topics in canine medicine, and is the recipient of various awards for her writing and dedication to animal health.

Photo Credits

Norvia Behling: pages 8 (bottom left), 12, 16 (top, center), 20, 25, 28, 33, 40, 44 (top right, center, and bottom), 31, 56, 57, 60, 65, 72, 84, 88 (top and bottom right), 89 (bottom); Kent and Donna Dannen: pages 2, 3, 4, 5, 8 (top left, center right, bottom right), 9, 13, 16 (bottom left and right), 17, 21, 24, 29, 32, 36, 37, 41, 44 (top left, bottom left), 45, 48 (top right, bottom left, and bottom right), 49, 53, 64, 68, 69, 73, 80, 81, 85, 88 (bottom left), 89 (top left and right), 92, 93; Tara Darling: pages 8 (top right), 48 (top left), 61, 77

Important Note

This book is concerned with selecting, keeping, and raising Fox Terriers. The publisher and the author think it is important to point out that the advice and information for Fox Terrier maintenance applies to healthy, normally developed animals. Anyone who acquires an adult dog or one from an animal shelter must consider that the animal may have behavioral problems and may, for example, bite without any visible provocation. Such anxiety biters are dangerous for the owner as well as the general public.

Caution is further advised in the association of children with dogs, in meetings with other dogs, and in exercising the dog without a leash.

Cover Photos

Front cover: Tara Darling; Back cover: Kent and Donna Dannen; Inside front and back covers: Kent and Donna Dannen

Acknowledgments

I would like to thank my husband, Jack Vanderlip, D.V.M., for his invaluable help as an expert consultant. As always, his ideas and suggestions contributed significantly to the quality of the manuscript and are greatly appreciated.

All inquiries should be addressed to:
Barron's Educational Series, Inc.
250 Wireless Boulevard
Hauppauge, NY 11788
http://www.barronseduc.com

International Standard Book No. 0-7641-1636-3

Library of Congress Catalog Card No. 00-054676

Library of Congress Cataloging-in-Publication Data
Vanderlip, Sharon Lynn.
  Fox terriers : everything about purchase, care, nutrition, and behavior / Sharon Vanderlip.
    p. cm. — (Complete pet owner's manual)
  ISBN 0-7641-1636-3
  1. Fox terriers. I. Title. II. Series.

SF429.F5 V36 2001
636.755—dc21   00-054676

Printed in Hong Kong

9 8 7 6 5 4 3 2 1